Women, work and demographic issues

Women, work and demographic issues

Report of an ILO/UNITAR Seminar
Tashkent, USSR, 11 - 19 October 1983

The research and technical co-operation activities which
were the subject of the seminar were financed by the
United Nations Fund for Population Activities (UNFPA)

International Labour Office   Geneva

ISBN 92-2-103886-6

First published 1984

Printed in Switzerland

Table of Contents

                                                                          Page

I.   BRIEF OUTLINE OF SEMINAR PROGRAMME AND
        PURPOSE   1

II.   OVERVIEW   5

III.   WOMEN'S ECONOMIC CONTRIBUTIONS   13

        1.   Measuring the female labour force   13
        2.   Rural case studies: India, Bangladesh and Egypt   20
        3.   Urban case studies: Cyprus, Mauritius, Nigeria
             and Ghana   25

IV.   WOMEN'S ROLES, FERTILITY AND FAMILY PLANNING
        IN HIGH FERTILITY AREAS   29

        1.   Bangladesh, India, Ghana and Nigeria   29
        2.   Uzbekistan (USSR), Colombia and Cuba   35

V.   FERTILITY AND FEMALE EMPLOYMENT IN LOW
        FERTILITY SOCIALIST COUNTRIES   41

VI.   INFORMATION FOR POLICY FORMULATION:
        UTILISATION OF RESEARCH FOR WOMEN'S AND
        POPULATION ISSUES   51

        1.   Agency and trade union perspectives   51
        2.   Government perspective   61

VII.   CONCLUSIONS   69

VIII.   SELECTED PAPERS   77

        1.   Female Labour Force Participation: ILO Research
             on Conceptual and Measurement Issues
             - R. Anker   79

2. Methodological Insights from Collaborative Indian Studies - M.E. Khan and S.K. Ghosh Dastidar   87

3. Mauritius: Women, Factory Employment and Fertility - C. Hein   93

4. Case Studies of Women's Roles, Fertility and Family Planning in High Fertility Countries: Ghana and Nigeria - C. Oppong   99

5. The Demographic Transition in Cuba: Women's Economic and Social Roles - A. Farnos and C. Alvarez-Lajonchere   107

6. The Female Employment Situation in the Soviet Union - S. Turchaninova   115

7. Government Perspectives on Utilisation of Research on Women and Population Issues in Pakistan - A. Inayatullah   120

8. Information for Policy Formulation in Hungary - K. Miltenyi   124

9. Government Perspectives and Utilisation of Research for Women's and Population Issues in Cyprus - E. Demetriades   128

10. Women, Work and Fertility in Uzbekistan   135

APPENDIX 1: List of Participants   141

APPENDIX 2: Seminar Programme   147

APPENDIX 3: List of Relevant ILO Publications   153

BRIEF OUTLINE OF PROGRAMME AND PURPOSE
OF THE SEMINAR

1.   The International Labour Office (ILO) and the United Nations Institute for Training and Research (UNITAR), in co-operation with the All-Union Central Council of Trade Unions of the USSR (AUCCTU), organised a seminar on Women, Work and Demographic Issues, which was held in Tashkent, USSR, from 11 to 19 October 1983.

2.   The aims of the seminar were:

(i)   Dissemination of the findings of research work carried out in a number of countries, as part of the UNFPA/ILO global research project "Women's Roles and Demographic Change" and of the ILO project "Economic Role of Women in Developing Countries: Improving Methods of Identification and Measurement", including related policy studies conducted under UNFPA/ILO country technical co-operation projects.

(ii)   Exchange of information and discussion on the methodologies employed in the above.

(iii)   Exchange of views and discussions between policy-makers and researchers on the impact of the UNFPA/ILO research work and studies on national policies, as well as implications for future research and action.

3.   There were 41 participants at the seminar.   A list appears in Appendix 1.   National researchers who had carried out studies under subcontract for the UNFPA/ILO global project "Women's Roles and Demographic Change" came from the following countries: Bangladesh, Brazil, Bulgaria, Canada, Cuba, Czechoslovakia, Egypt, Ghana, Hungary, India, Nigeria, the USA, and the USSR.   There were also government participants from Ministries or Offices of Planning, Population, Social Affairs, Labour and Statistics in Bangladesh, Bulgaria, Cuba, Cyprus, Hungary, Jordan, People's Democratic Republic of Yemen, Pakistan, and the USSR most of whom are involved in ILO technical co-operation projects concerning women, population, human resources, and development planning.   In addition, there were two consultants drawn from trade union circles in Bangladesh and India as designated by the ILO's Workers Group of the Governing Body.   Officials from the ILO and specialists from the Soviet Union also participated.   Participants thus came from governments, trade unions, and various types of research organisations and from countries with different socio-economic systems and at different stages of development.   The discussions were enriched by this diversity, and demonstrated that fruitful exchanges can take place across political, economic and social divides on matters of common concern.

4. At the opening of the seminar Mrs. Makhmudova, President of the Uzbek Trade Union Council, was in the chair. Participants were welcomed to the Republic of Uzbekistan and to the city of Tashkent by the Vice President of the Council of Ministers of the Uzbek SSR and by the Deputy Mayor of Tashkent.

It was pointed out that in the Republic of Uzbekistan very high value is attached to women's roles both as mothers and as workers, and that many Uzbek women are able to combine working and having large families. How effectively these roles are combined is shown by the high birth rate and high female labour force participation rate among Uzbek women.

5. In his opening address, Mr. Kailas Doctor, Chief, Population and Labour Policies Branch, ILO, expressed his thanks to the Government of the Soviet Union, and especially to the Council of Ministers of the Uzbek SSR and the City Council of Tashkent, for their hospitality. He also thanked the All-Union Central Council of Trade Unions for financing and seeing to all the practical arrangements for the seminar, and the Uzbek Republican Trade Union Council for hosting the seminar in Tashkent.

Mr. Doctor expressed his appreciation for the co-operation of UNITAR, which had made a contribution towards the seminar costs, and regretted that no-one from this organisation had been able to attend because of the meeting of the UN General Assembly.

6. Mr. Richard Anker then presented an overview of the UNFPA/ILO research programme on "Women's Roles and Demographic Change", as given in the next section of this report.

7. Eight half-day sessions were subsequently devoted to the presentation of papers discussing policy-oriented research on women, work, and fertility (see Appendix 2 for details of seminar programme). Each session also included comments on the papers by the discussants for that session followed by an open discussion among all participants. Sections III-VI of this report describe each session, with brief summaries of the papers presented, the main comments made by the discussants, and the main points raised in the general discussion. In order that the reader may profit from the details given in at least some of the papers, Section VIII of the report presents approximately one paper from each of the sessions.

8. In order to draw up a set of conclusions, seminar participants decided to nominate a drafting committee with one representative appointed by participants from each geographic region. The committee membership was as follows:

Eastern Europe	Zdenek Pavlik, Czechoslovakia
USSR	Rimma Dmitrieva, USSR
Africa	Lawrence Adeokun, Nigeria
Middle East	Noor Saleh, PDRY
Latin America	Mary Castro, Brazil
Asia	M. Ejazuddin Khan, India
North America	Eva Mueller, USA

The drafting committee elected Z. Pavlik as chairperson and E. Mueller as rapporteur. ILO staff acted as resource persons for the drafting committee.

9. The conclusions proposed by the drafting committee were discussed by all the participants in two plenary sessions. The final version constitutes Section VII of this report.

10. The closing session of the seminar was graced by the presence of various officials of the Uzbek Republican Trade Union Council. Mr. Akram Tashmatov, Secretary, Uzbek Republican Trade Union Council, represented Mrs. Makhmudova on this occasion.

On behalf of the seminar participants, Mr. Evros Demetriades expressed appreciation to the AUCCTU and the Trade Union Council of the Uzbek Republic for the enjoyable stay in the Soviet Union made possible by their efficient organis-ation and generous hospitality.

Mr. Doctor thanked the participants for their contributions to the seminar which had permitted a lively and fruitful debate to take place. Mr. Doctor also thanked the hosts for the excellent organisation of the external programme of the seminar and their lavish, warm hospitality. In addition, he expressed his appreciation of the excellent arrangements made for publicising the proceedings of the seminar through the press, radio and television. He concluded that the atmosphere of goodwill which surrounded the seminar had made the participants' stay in Tashkent, city of friendship and peace, a very memorable one.

11. On their return to Moscow, the seminar participants received an address from Mrs. Alexandra Biryukova, Secretary AUCCTU, on labour, employment, social security, and demo-graphic issues, especially those aspects relevant to women's work. This was followed by a question and answer session.

Eastern Europe .... Zdenek Paylik, Czechoslovakia
USSR .... Rimma Dmitrieva, USSR
Africa .... Lawrence Adeokun, Nigeria
Middle East .... Anne Bailey, PDRY
Latin America .... Mario Castro, Brazil
Asia .... M. Fazzudin Khan, India
North America .... Eva Mueller, USA

II. OVERVIEW

This seminar presented an unusually good opportunity for researchers and policy-makers to discuss their mutual interests and concerns.   The UNFPA/ILO research programme which formed the basis of the seminar was conceived as an integrated research and action programme on population and labour policy issues.   It is not surprising, therefore, that the researchers and policy-makers involved in the programme (and who comprised the majority of seminar participants) are firm believers in the feasibility and usefulness of policy research and, in fact, often combine the functions of researcher and policy-maker in their professional activities.   The multidisciplinary approach to studying women, work, and population issues was also reflected in the wide range of disciplines from which seminar participants were drawn: demography, economics, statistics, sociology, anthropology, medicine, geography, and psychology.

Relations between researchers and policy-makers have not always been as good as they might be.   Policy-makers tend to regard research as an intellectual activity of relatively little interest to them;   in contrast they see themselves as dealing with practical problems, political considerations, and the complexities of everyday life, both in the world outside and within their own bureaucracies.   Researchers, on the other hand, tend to see policy-makers as hopefully well-intentioned bureaucrats who make decisions on the basis of little or no knowledge.

Although there are grains of truth in such views (if there were not they would not be taken so seriously by those concerned), they are not the whole truth.   As the seminar deliberations show, there should be a complementary relationship between researcher and policy-maker: while the policy-maker needs information for effective planning, the social science researcher needs to be concerned with practical policy-relevant issues if her/his work is to be meaningful and useful.

The UNFPA/ILO research programme on "Women's Roles and Demographic Change" was begun in 1978 as part of the Population and Labour Policies component of the ILO's World Employment Programme.   In 1978 this programme had been in existence for six years, and had concentrated most of its effort so far on the modelling of economic-demographic relationships in large-scale macro simulation models, dubbed Bachue after a Colombian goddess of love, fertility and harmony between nature and mankind.   The ILO's technical assistance activities in the population field had been going on for a similar length of time and had largely concentrated on population-education/family welfare activities for workers in industrial or rural development/ co-operative settings.

But shifts in emphasis were taking place.   On the research side there was a feeling that while macro simulation models were useful, they provided only one highly simplified perspective on reality. It was felt to be important to undertake in-depth investigations of key economic-demographic relationships, and to make use of techniques and insights from disciplines other than economics. As a result, research projects were set up on "Women's Roles and Demographic Change" in 1978, on "Population Mobility, Employment and Policy Design" in 1979, and on "Population, Labour and Poverty" in 1980.

On the technical assistance side, the main emphasis of the new programme (begun in 1976) was on introducing population concerns into development and employment planning through the establishment of teams of regional advisers for Africa, Asia, the Middle East, and Latin America through UNFPA-funded country planning projects. This technical assistance programme (entitled "Population, Human Resources and Development Planning") bridged the gap between research and action, between the production of quality research reports and their utilisation.

The "Women's Roles and Demographic Change" project, with which this seminar is concerned, thus grew out of a research project which needed to be policy-oriented while feeding into and being mutually supportive of country-level activities developed under the technical assistance programme. In terms of subject area, this new research project was ideal. Women's issues were of concern to most governments in the world, due to the growing awareness of inequalities between men and women. Inequalities in employment and in the labour market were chief among these concerns, as is attested by the formation of a unit in the ILO on women's issues, which is described in Section VI. As regards population issues, there was (and still is) a general consensus that population growth rates are determined to a large extent by the situation of women, their roles and their status and that family reproductive constraints have a major effect on the labour market situation of women.

The ILO research programme began with generous funding from UNFPA - which had itself broadened its own perspective on population issues, among other things setting up a unit on women's issues. Its main objectives were as follows:

(i)   To measure and demonstrate to policy-makers and to informed public opinion the important economic contribution made by women.

(ii)   To establish the effect on women's productive activities of important developmental changes concerning, for example, industrial structures and job markets, agricultural technology, labour-saving investments, and educational opportunities.

(iii)   To investigate the effect on women's position of government and non-government measures aimed at improving women's status, such as educational programmes, the setting up of co-operatives, income-generating schemes, and improved job opportunities for women.

(iv)   To study the effect on women's productive activities of changes in marriage, migration, fertility, mortality, and family structure.

(v)   To study this relationship in reverse, that is, to see how changes in the productive activities of women affect marriage, migration, fertility, mortality, and their relative position in the family.

In order to accomplish these objectives, an inter-disciplinary approach was adopted, since it was felt that questions related to women's roles could not be understood from the relatively narrow perspective provided by any one particular discipline. The decision was therefore made to undertake four broad interrelated types of study: (i) socio-anthropological studies; (ii) studies using household sample surveys; (iii) studies or urban labour markets; and (iv) methodological development of appropriate research techniques and tools. These four approaches were in fact integrated in three major studies carried out in Bangladesh, Egypt and India. Several of the seminar papers are by persons directing such studies, M. Elahi, A. Shoukry, and M.E. Khan.

It should be noted that major consideration was given to methodological issues in order to increase our knowledge of how to carry out policy-oriented research, thus improving the position of the ILO for advising nationals conducting such research; that considerable attention was given to broadening the measurement of economic activity, to include many hard-working women who are all too often recorded as "housewives" on survey questionnaires and in national statistics; and that attention was given to the effects of developmental and governmental interventions.

Sections III, IV and V of this report are based on the papers presented at the seminar by researchers who have worked within the UNFPA/ILO research programme on "Women's Roles and Demographic Change". The papers deal with a wide range of subjects and very different levels of economic development.

Section III is concerned with the participation of women in economic life: how it is (and is not) measured; how it is (and is not) valued in the official statistics; and appropriate methodologies for understanding its interaction with demographic variables such as fertility and family size. The first session covered in Section III dealt with the well-known problem of under-estimation of female labour force activity in surveys and censuses in the Third World. Anker reviewed the reasons for this under-estimation and described those activities under the ILO's research programme aimed at finding solutions to these problems. Oppong described the interdisciplinary nature of the ILO research programme and then went on to give examples of the insights which can be provided by the in-depth qualitative case study approach. The third paper in this session, by Khan, complemented the other two, since it reported on some of the insights to be gained from the several studies in India on which he is collaborating with the ILO, which use methodologies and approaches developed under the ILO programme in collaboration with his own organisation.

The second session was concerned with the economic activities and opportunities of women in rural areas of the Third World. All three of the country studies are based on preliminary results and observations from comparable ILO-supported studies under way in Bangladesh, Egypt and India. To carry out these major studies, several anthropologists from each country each lived for a year in a different village. Over this one-year period they observed and recorded behaviour as well as talking to women and men about how they used their time, what they did, decision-making, health, fertility, family planning, etc. Household surveys were carried out in the surrounding villages, using approximately 1,000 women and men. A unique aspect of this research is that the survey questionnaires and the field guides for the case study were developed specifically to complement each other - the surveys to provide quantitative data for a relatively large number of families and the in-depth case studies to provide highly accurate information on the reasons/ mechanism for observed relationships and on sensitive or difficult topics for which survey questions are not suited (as well as a quality check on the survey data).

The third session focused on women in the urban labour market - on factors such as the types of job held, pay levels, recruitment and promotion practices, fertility levels, and family constraints. The two West African countries reported on (Ghana and Nigeria) are countries in which women have always been very active in areas such as petty trading and agriculture; they are also labour surplus economies. The other two countries (Cyprus and Mauritius) are very different, relatively small island countries. It is interesting to see how sex discrimination and segregation differ in such countries. What makes these papers especially interesting is that all four are based on primary data, and that both employers and employees were interviewed in order to understand how male and female workers are recruited, paid, fired, and so on.

Section IV focuses on the main factors relating to health, family planning and fertility in developing countries. One paper described the ways in which women and girls are discriminated against in health care in rural India; this, too, is based on preliminary results from the major Indian study briefly described above. India is one of the few countries with higher mortality rates for females than for males, and this paper showed just how pervasive sex discrimination in health care in India is. The paper on Ghana and Nigeria provided additional illustrations of the sorts of insight which qualitative case study research is able to provide. The Colombian study highlighted the situation of a group of women (female heads of households) who are widely recognised to be the "poorest of the poor". This group clearly deserves special attention, as the Colombian paper very forcefully argued.

The papers on Uzbekistan and the USSR had special relevance for this seminar. Not only did the seminar take place in Uzbekistan, but Uzbekistan also has an unusual demographic situation. Among Uzbek nationals, fertility rates are high. Yet all the conditions for a low fertility rate would seem to be present: life expectancy is high, education levels are high, and almost all women in urban areas work outside the home.

The two papers on Cuba summarised in Sections IV and V were also of great interest, since the fertility rate is at present very low in Cuba (below replacement), even though it is a developing country. The first paper, which dealt with the reasons for this unexpectedly rapid decline in fertility, was of particular interest to those from developing countries concerned with high population growth rates. The second Cuban paper dealt with sex education, since Cuba is undertaking a major sex education programme partly because of the age-fertility profile in Cuba, which is very young. Since teenage fertility is a serious health, social, labour and women's problem in many areas of the world, the Cuban experience of this new programme provides some important lessons.

Section V is concerned with low fertility socialist countries - Bulgaria, Cuba, Czechoslovakia, Hungary and the USSR - more specifically with the trend, level, distribution and determinants of female employment and fertility. Fertility rates in these countries are mostly around replacement level and female labour force participation rates high (women comprise approximately half the labour force in the European socialist countries). This situation is very different from that in developing countries such as those discussed in Sections III and IV. Nevertheless, there is much that high fertility countries can learn from the experiences of the low fertility countries. Socialist countries view population policy as an integral part of social and economic policy, recognising that social and economic policies interact with population dynamics. They attempt to reduce the conflict women experience between their roles as workers and mother - thus facilitating the combination of the two roles. The policies adopted to this end include the granting of paid maternity leave, extended unpaid maternity leave, and sick leave to care for children, and the provision of crèches, child-care allowances, etc. Observations were made in these papers on how the many incentives and socially desirable policies enacted in these countries affect fertility and female employment.

Sections VI and VII report on the sessions where participants who are policy-makers or administrators (often with research backgrounds) gave us the benefit of their experience. In these sessions, participants explained how research and action can be effectively combined, and how research can be made as relevant to policy-making as possible. Much can be learned from this experience. It is well-known that research is not as fully utilised as it should be by policy-makers and that researchers are not sensitive enough to the need for effective communication with policy-makers: there should be constant interaction with policy-makers beginning with the inception of the programme, and results should be presented as straight-forwardly as possible.

The last sessions were devoted to establishing the major conclusions of the seminar regarding appropriate research approaches and methodologies, utilisation of research, and areas for future research. The common orientations agreed by both policy-makers and researchers at the seminar should provide useful guidelines for other researchers and policy-makers.

The UN Decade for Women will soon be drawing to a close, but this does not mean that research related to women should end or that policy measures lose any of their importance. If anything, the research conducted throughout this decade has shown that much still needs to be done to improve the quality of life of women and that the complexities of population and women's issues are still far from being adequately understood. The world-wide commitment to equality between men and women as a basic human right must not slacken.

SEMINAR PROCEEDINGS

III. WOMEN'S ECONOMIC CONTRIBUTIONS

1.   Measuring the female labour force

<u>Chairperson</u>: Richard Anker

<u>Papers</u>:

a.   Anker, Richard - "Female labour force participation: ILO research on conceptual measurement issues" (reproduced in Section VIII)

b.   Oppong, Christine - "Usefulness   of   qualitative   micro approaches"

c.   Khan, M. Ejazuddin and Dastidar, S.K. Ghosh - "Methodological insights from collaborative Indian studies" (reproduced in Section VIII)

<u>Discussants</u>:   Eva Mueller
                          Lawrence Adeokun

     This session focused mainly on the problems of defining and measuring labour force activity and the need for multidisciplinary research approaches. It is widely recognised that currently available statistics from the developing world are inaccurate and often grossly under-report the economic activities of women. It is important to have more accurate data on women's economic activities both to provide improved estimates of the labour force for planning purposes and to enable researchers to relate women's economic activities to their fertility.

Papers

a. In his paper, Richard Anker suggested three factors which are important in the under-reporting of women's labour force participation. Firstly, the international definition of labour force activity and its interpretation at the national level has meant that certain economic activities typically performed by women are excluded from the definition of labour force and from national income accounts. Secondly, most surveys are designed by men and conducted by male interviewers who interview male respondents. The stereotype of women as "housewives" may be stronger among men, so causing women's economic activities to be unreported. Thirdly, the simplistic nature of survey questions concerning labour force activity, which seek to divide the population into economically active and inactive groups, encourages simplistic replies and fails to recognise the complexity of the underlying situation.

The UNFPA/ILO research programme on "Women's Roles and Demographic Change" has been concerned with developing ways of improving the measurement of female labour force activity and increasing understanding of its relationship to demographic variables such as fertility, family planning, and health. A multidisciplinary approach was adopted which included both the individual and household survey questionnaires favoured by economists and statisticians and the in-depth qualitative case study approach favoured by anthropologists. Thus, "model" questionnaires (Anker, 1980), a quantitative-qualitative study design (Anker, 1982), a case study framework (Oppong, 1980), and case study field guides (Oppong and Church, 1981; Nag, Anker and Khan, 1982) were developed. Major multidisciplinary studies are currently being undertaken in India, Egypt and Bangladesh, using several different data collection techniques.

In addition, the ILO is currently conducting studies in India and Egypt, in collaboration with local institutions, to evaluate the effect of the interviewer's sex, the respondent's sex, self versus proxy respondents, and the type of question-naire on the reporting of female labour force activity (see Anker, 1983b for a detailed description). The results will help to improve the collection of such data in national censuses and labour force surveys where detailed activity/time use surveys are not possible. The new questionnaires being developed and tested are relatively easy to use, require relatively little inter-view time, and avoid building in preconceived concepts and definitions of labour force participation.

The ILO research programme is also looking at the problems of evaluating unpaid household and subsistence activities (see Goldschmidt-Clermont, 1982). Such activities are usually carried out by women and/or children and tend to be overlooked in definitions of labour force participation and national income accounts statistics.

b.   In her paper, Christine Oppong looked at the decision to make the UNFPA/ILO programme interdisciplinary and to use several information-gathering techniques.   She pointed out that it was taken at a time in the seventies when scholars and policy-makers, concerned with the processes, causes and consequences of economic and demographic change, were increasingly coming to realise that analysis of census and large-scale sample survey data is alone inadequate to provide understanding, either of the dynamic interactions involved or of the ideal inputs and inter-ventions needed to bring about desired changes and developments.

She summarised three case studies conducted within the framework of the UNFPA/ILO project on "Women's Roles and Demographic Change" to show how research methods which may be called micro or qualitative can be used to increase under-standing of women's occupational and reproductive roles.   In certain instances, the classificatory framework used to systematise the collection and analysis of data was that elaborated by Oppong and Church (1981).   It includes the seven roles women play in social life as (1) mothers, (2) workers outside the home, (3) wives, (4) domestic workers in the home, (5) kin, (6) community members, and (7) self-actualising individuals.   Associated with each role is an array of data on activities, resources (including time, knowledge, money and material goods) and their acquisition, allocation, management and control, decision-making, and power relationships with significant others.   This framework assists in the systematic collection and analysis of data on role behaviour, role resources, and role expectations, including norms/rules and laws, values, beliefs and perceptions.

The first case study was done by Nadia Atif, an Egyptian anthropologist, who carried out a qualitative in-depth study of married women workers in the carpet factory of the Co-operative Society for Cottage Industries in the Egyptian town of Mehalla al Kubra.

She describes the constraints to women's labour force participation imposed by kin control and perceptions of female honour.   A critical issue she observed and documented was the extent to which, for married women, the factory is the main area for individually selected social relationships;   the factory system also offers the main opportunity in women's lives for informal exchange of information and advice on health, contraception and child-care and for the discussion of family size goals and family planning practices - topics which women often cannot and do not discuss with husbands.   She discovered that although none of the women studied had visited a family planning clinic after the birth of the first child, the majority took the contraceptive pill as advised by workmates or female relatives.   Doctors were not consulted for advice.

In the second case study, Patricia Lynch with Hoda Fahmy (1983 and 1984) provides ethnographic evidence about a set of 11 Moslem women craft workers in an Egyptian community, relating the women's work to their child-bearing and child-rearing activities. One significant finding is that there is an apparent connection between women's involvement in household production and pregnancy. One explanation given by the women themselves for bearing so many children is that they feel the need for additional child labour to increase their productivity.

The authors point to the domination of husbands in family planning matters when they are also economically dominant in the household. Where women are involved in production and financially independent, family planning is not necessarily the decision of the husband alone.

The third case study, Leela Gulati's study of Kerala women (Gulati, 1983 and in press), focuses upon the economic and demographic impact new methods of fishing and preserving fish have on women in three communities in India. Three villages, a total of 30 households and 30 women, were selected for in-depth description and analysis, and ethnographic methods of data collection were used in addition to survey and archival evidence.

The changes documented include women's increased partici-pation in work, the lowering of female infant and maternal mortality, the lowering of fertility, and the widespread adoption of female sterilisation. Accompanying changes include an increase in the domestic influence of women and increased partici pation in domestic activities of men; these have been related in other studies to similar economic and demographic changes. The author considers one of the most dramatic changes to be that in family size, which is linked both to the lowering of infant mortality and to the widespread availability and use of hospital facilities.

c. M. Ejazuddin Khan of Operations Research Group, who is one of the collaborators for studies in India, commented on his experience of combining a sample survey with village case studies when studying the interactions between demographic factors and employment. The concern to develop a new methodology which could be used in different socio-economic settings made this work especially challenging for him.

Khan's experience in India shows the usefulness of an integrated approach. The detailed information provided by the case studies on the dynamics of decision-making processes could not have been obtained from survey data alone. On the other hand, one cannot generalise from case studies on their own because of the small sample size. The usefulness of this sort of approach in obtaining policy-relevant data is now being appreciated by policy-makers in India in many institutions and ministries (Indian Council of Medical Research, Ministry of Health and Family Welfare, Central Statistical Office).

The integrated approach is not without problems, however. It requires a careful organisation and dedicated social scientists willing to live in village communities for long periods of time. Finding such persons is difficult - particularly women. During this study some women joined and left, which caused considerable delays.

Collecting time use data every 15 days was not liked by villagers. At first, small gifts were given to the informant or her children, but in the process villagers became rather demanding. A more successful approach was to do some social work which would benefit the community - for example giving help with getting treatment at government clinics, getting a water tap connected in the village. Another problem with the collection of time use data was that villagers did not have a clear concept of time, so the information given was rather crude and approximate.

Khan's experience in India suggested that it was unnecessary to live continuously in the village for an entire year. It was important in the first two or three months for establishing rapport with informants, but subsequently he felt periodic visits (about 10 days a month) would suffice for collecting data.

The establishment of good rapport over a period of time was found to increase the frankness of informants, particularly on sensitive issues such as family planning and communication between spouses. Some informants in fact corrected their original replies to questions on later occasions. When asked why they had given a wrong reply previously they said, "Would you tell all about your family to a stranger on the first day without knowing his/her motive?"

Discussion

The discussant, Eva Mueller, expressed her pleasure that the programme at the ILO was trying to improve methods for collecting labour force data. However, data collection is a very difficult area and she did not think progress would be easy. She agreed with the ILO's conclusion that a detailed time use approach to improving national labour force surveys was not really viable, and thought that the current direction of research was more practical. She also felt that the suggestion that there should be several definitions of labour force participation was a step in the right direction because of the inherent imprecision (especially in the Third World) involved in dividing activities into labour force and non-labour force activities; it also takes into consideration the fact that many service activities which are frequently considered to be labour force activities in developed countries may be performed in the home in less developed countries.

The discussant also expressed an appreciation for the comprehensive, holistic and multidisciplinary approach adopted by the UNFPA/ILO programme, though she expressed some scepticism about the practicality of combining methodologies.

With respect to time use data, while agreeing that such data could be useful, the discussant expressed certain reservations as to whether it was always a significant improvement over other types of data which require less time, effort and expense to collect and analyse. Additionally, problems of classifying activities and recording simultaneous activities mean that time use data is rather approximate and difficult to interpret.

Mueller also emphasised that time use data may overestimate the economic contribution made by women's unpaid work. This is because women are allocated the least productive tasks, and their productivity is accordingly not commensurate with the amount of time and effort expended. This aspect of the sexual division of labour within many societies complicates any evaluation of women's economic contribution, since total value is the product of productivity per hour and the number of hours worked.

The second discussant, Lawrence Adeokun, noted that the papers of Anker and Oppong indicated the strong ILO concern with the methodological problems of accurately documenting and analysing women's work and related demographic issues, primarily in the developing countries but paying due attention to international comparability of methods, materials and findings.

Among the reasons mentioned by Anker for the inadequacies of present systems of surveying female labour force participation, the discussant emphasised the use of inappropriately worded and constructed questions, which lead to inaccurate responses. This was one area where the discussant felt that improvements were possible and therefore very appropriate as part of the ILO's current research activities. He felt the problem was a cumulative one. It starts when concepts and hypotheses are formulated by researchers in one particular language for the study of societies embracing a wide range of tongues and cultures. It is compounded by the mechanism of funding research, which often precludes elaborate pilot studies and requires the use of "core questionnaires" in the name of "international comparability". By the time a half-literate, poorly-trained interviewer administers a highly technical questionnaire to the illiterate respondent the damage is done as far as "accuracy" is concerned. Sometimes parsimony in the construction of the questionnaire is carried too far: at times three questions can be better than one.

The use of a detailed activity/time use approach has the advantage of avoiding the bias of a priori assumptions. It can also improve the accuracy of female labour force data. Although Adeokun agreed that the cost of collecting detailed activity/time use data restricts its use to small samples and to serving as quality checks for larger surveys, such data can provide the basis of a concise but comprehensive activity list for large questionnaire surveys.

The discussant supported Oppong's emphasis on the importance of qualitiative micro approaches. Quantitative survey studies often fail to provide an understanding of "dynamic interactions" or "mechanisms". Hypotheses link variables into causal and measurable relationships. It is fashionable and "scientific" to collect data to measure and test relationships between variables. The snag is that hypotheses often do not identify "mechanism(s)". A study may well reveal an association between certain activities and the adoption of family planning and establish a causal link between the two, but to understand the mechanism or dynamic interaction it is necessary to put the relationship into a temporal and specific context. Asking relevant questions, observing and interpreting correctly in the given situation, forms the basis of understanding the mechanism. One example is the case of the Ishan women for whom trading was related to use of contraception; the reason was that trading resulted in frequent periods of absence from the rural community in a nearby but large urban centre where the women could seek contraceptives in anonymity, away from the prying neighbour.

In the open discussion, various problems were mentioned concerning the definition of labour force activity. For example, what about the activities of women which are part of a process which eventually becomes market-oriented? And what meaning does labour force activity have in a subsistence economy? It was suggested that existing definitions have a sex bias which tends to include men and exclude women. It was generally agreed that the issues involved are complex and that the application of existing definitions is often difficult and confusing.

Participants generally expressed the view that the combination of qualitative and quantitative methods, as in the UNFPA/ILO research programme, was a useful approach. On the one hand, survey data was felt by some to be essential as a basis for policy decisions since it covers a representative sample using reasonably objective, standard procedures. On the other hand, it was recognised that survey data alone can be misleading. The example was given of research in Egypt where women's answers to survey questions about their work were different from what they could actually be observed doing. Furthermore, even at best, survey data do not provide insights into the reasons for a relationship, or "the mechanisms". Participants therefore agreed that in-depth research using small samples is important both as a quality check on larger surveys and for improving understanding of the relations between variables. For certain types of research question, micro studies are in any case more appropriate than large-scale survey methods. However, the general concensus was that for policy formulation, micro studies were by themselves insufficiently representative.

There was considerable discussion about one specific method of obtaining micro-level data - that of time use studies. It was agreed that there are advantages to this method, especially since it avoids the bias of a priori assumptions as to what constitutes labour force activity. However, it was agreed that this data was in fact approximate and sometimes difficult to interpret.

2. Rural case studies: India, Bangladesh and Egypt

Chairperson: Alexandre Pervouchine

Papers:

a.   Khan, M. Ejazuddin, Singh, R. and Abidi, N.F. - "Women in the handloom industry: A case study of handloom centres in Uttar Pradesh"

b.   Elahi, K. Maumood - "Government programmes for women in Bangladesh villages"

c.   Shoukry, Aliaa - "Women's roles and demographic change in Egypt: Experience of participant field research"

Discussants: Attiya Inayatullah
Eugenia Date-Bah

Programmes designed to improve the lot of rural women, such as income-generating activities, introduction of new technology, and so on, do not always have positive results. The papers on Bangladesh and India in this session discussed the reasons for the rather limited success of certain projects in these countries. The Egyptian paper described the difficulties of obtaining an accurate picture of women's economic activities in rural areas and, on the basis of field work experience in Egypt, argued for the usefulness of in-depth observation as opposed to survey techniques.

Papers

a. The paper by Ejazuddin Khan et al. described how in Uttar Pradesh, a northern state of India, the government, in collaboration with an international agency (not the ILO), opened 14 handloom centres. These centres were intended to provide employment for weaver families who had lost their looms in floods. It was planned that 70 per cent of this employment would go to women and children of these families. The project did not achieve these goals, however. Workers did not come to work in families as had been expected, and in some centres many of the looms were not used at all. Most disturbingly, the majority of workers were men rather than women and children, as originally planned.

There were numerous reasons for the low participation of women in the project, and these were not taken into account in the feasibility study. Women, in fact, have little free time available for working outside the home. (The crèches provided by the handloom centres were little used as they were considered to provide poor services.) Furthermore, Muslim and high caste Hindu women have to observe purdah, and cannot work in the same room as men, while among lower caste Hindus weaving is not traditionally done by women. Finally, many of the weaver families were in debt to private agents, and so had to continue working with these agents rather than joining the project.

The paper concluded that a project which is in conflict with the prevalent socio-cultural values cannot be expected to succeed. In the context described, it was unrealistic to attempt to bring women to workplaces outside their homes - especially at the wages being paid. Nor did the project include women in the planning process or take into account their problems and felt needs. This is a common and well-known reason for the failure of such projects, yet the mistake was repeated in this case.

b. The second paper, by Maumood Elahi, concerned Bangladesh, where the number of women's programmes sponsored by the government has increased greatly in the last decade. The Government of Bangladesh is at present attaching increased importance to the role of women in development in general and in the workforce in particular. In addition to alleviating poverty and improving the welfare of the rural poor, this policy is expected to reduce fertility. Indeed, the National Population Policy of Bangladesh is now viewed as "an integrated component of total social mobilisation and national development efforts". At the same time, the spread of family planning, resulting in lower fertility, is viewed as a means by which women can be released from their pressing household duties so as to contribute more effectively to the national work effort.

The government programmes for women may be divided into three broad categories: literacy programmes, the provision of health and family planning services, and income-generating projects. Income-generating projects have been the most common but have also tended to have rather limited success.

Some of the problems, identified by a study of 214 women's organisations, are related to the non-availability of capital, the irregular supply of raw materials, the need for skilled trainers, and the lack of dependable marketing facilities. Other factors were also being investigated as part of an in-depth ILO study on "Rural Fertility and Female Economic Activity in Bangladesh". Elahi noted some tentative observations from this study. He pointed out the way in which most government-sponsored programmes for women are prepared by extension officers from outside and then imposed upon a particular group of women. The local resource base and existing skills are hardly considered when a programme is being developed. On the other hand, groups of women in a village with certain skills, in cottage industries or handicrafts for example, are very rarely covered by any government programme. Finally, local leadership and organisation have not been developed under the present programme structure; for this reason alone, its impact cannot be expected to be very lasting.

c. The paper by Aliaa Shoukry on research in rural areas of Egypt demonstrated the difficulties of obtaining valid information about women. Answers to questionnaires about the economic activities of women were found not to correspond with what the women were in fact doing. In general, the replies to questionnaires tended to underestimate the amount of work women did. Some women claimed to do no agricultural work but were frequently observed going to the fields to help their husbands and children.

The author also pointed out that questionnaire replies gave little idea of how women's activities are adjusted to seasonal changes or to events like pregnancy, migration of husband, and the introduction of new agricultural practices. However, through participant observation for a year or more, research teams are able to document changes in the work and activities of female informants (as Shoukry and her colleagues are doing in the project on "Women's Roles and Demographic Change in Egypt").

This paper thus illustrated the importance of in-depth observation for obtaining information on women's activities and for understanding the situation of women within a given socio-economic context.

Discussion

The discussant, Eugenia Date-Bah, commented on projects to introduce improved technology for rural women. She suggested that many have failed because governments and international agencies have not learned from past experience the complexity of the situation and the importance of adopting a holistic approach. One must consider not only the technology itself but also the economic and socio-cultural factors which will influence the success of its introduction. Even when a new technology has been adopted, it has sometimes increased rather than decreased the women's work burden, and sometimes the men have made use of the more productive techniques and women have lost a traditional source of income.

The discussant suggested some factors which she felt were responsible for the failure of projects which may be overlooked in project design:

(i) Familiarisation and training with the new technology was inadequate.

(ii) The traditional sexual division of labour within the society was not adequately studied and taken into account.

(iii) The felt needs of the women were not ascertained.

(iv) The usual scheduling and location of activities were not considered.

(v) Supplies of raw materials and spare parts were not ensured.

(vi) Decision-making and control over income within the family were overlooked.

(vii) Access to credit and marketing (where relevant) were not ensured.

The second discussant, Attiya Inayatullah, also emphasised the need to study women's and population issues in broader contexts, as was being done in the ILO projects, rather than in isolation. Projects for rural women must take into account the total context of agrarian societies, which are often characterised by geographic isolation, traditional attitudes, a well-defined sexual division of labour, and a well-entrenched local leadership. One must also be careful about internal feuds, which may mean that different segments of the local population have different interests.

The discussant suggested that researchers should be careful in their approach to traditional practices and give them the respect they merit. Of course, some practices which are exploitative, such as using women as beasts of burden, should be questioned. Programmes in rural areas must take full account of the existing situation. There may sometimes be a rich heritage of folkcraft and cottage industries carried on by women which could be developed. The seasonal nature of agricultural work may also mean that women have free time at certain times of year but not others. Apart from income-generating projects, the basic needs of women and children, the most vulnerable groups, should be met through appropriate health provision, waste disposal and water supply. Projects for women should include the development of leadership within the local group, including training where appropriate.

In the discussion which followed, the participants emphasised the need for a multi-faceted, comprehensive approach to the introduction of change. The importance of collaboration at both government and grass-roots levels was also stressed.

In general, participants felt that successful change would need to be a slow process, which did not disrupt the structure of the society. It was pointed out, however, that there may be a certain contradiction between the goals of promoting social change and preserving the traditional culture. If, for example, there are positive social benefits to be gained from encouraging women to work outside the home, should income-generating projects accept the traditional pattern of work within the home?

The session tended to dwell on projects which had not succeeded and the failure to learn from past experience, partly because these were the projects reported in the papers. Participants felt that more attention should be given to successful projects and the lessons to be learned from them.

3.　　Urban case studies:　Cyprus, Mauritius, Nigeria and Ghana

Chairperson:　Richard Anker

Papers

a.　Demetriades, Evros - "Tapping the female labour reserve in Cyprus"

b.　Hein, Catherine - "Women, factory employment and fertility" (reproduced in Section VIII)

c.　Adeokun, Lawrence - "Cause of sex discrimination in an urban labour market:　Women's work in a Nigerian city"

d.　Date-Bah, Eugenia - "Women's work in a Ghanaian city"

Discussant:　Mary Castro

Equality of opportunity and treatment in employment and related matters such as education and training has long been a basic principle of the ILO.　As part of the UNFPA/ILO research programme, studies were conducted in developing countries to determine what proportion of women are employed in the "modern" or "formal" sector, and how they are treated.　The relationship of such employment to women's fertility was also a concern of these field studies.　As well as documenting sexual inequalities, these studies sought to understand the reasons for them and interviewed both employers and employees to obtain their points of view.　The papers presented in this session are based on detailed studies which will be published in a forth-coming book edited by Anker and Hein, Sex discrimination and sex segregation in urban labour markets of the Third World.

Papers

a.   The papers on Mauritius and Cyprus described situations where the demand for women workers is high. In Cyprus, Evros Demetriades pointed out, there is a shortage of female labour for labour-intensive exporting industries, and surveys were undertaken to investigate ways in which currently inactive women could be drawn into the labour force. A survey of the employment status of women showed that there is marked occupational segregation in Cyprus (House, 1982b and 1983). Many jobs are conceived as "male" or "female" preserves for which members of the opposite sex are not considered. This is especially apparent in certain professional and supervisory occupations, which are reserved for men, and in some low-skilled blue-collar jobs for which only women are thought fit. Women are paid less even where they work side by side with men doing the same job. Furthermore, their chances of on-the-job or out-of-firm training, and promotion, are much lower than those of men.

The major problems with female workers, often cited by employers, are: absenteeism, pregnancy and maternity leave, inability to accept responsibility, and lack of interest or motivation in their work. The results of the employers' survey in Cyprus confirmed that ever-married women are slightly more prone to absenteeism, but the employers' beliefs that there is a greater turnover of jobs among women were not justified. Measures to improve the skills of women, to provide greater equality of opportunity and treatment in employment, and to help women combine work outside the home with child-care responsibilities, are all being undertaken as part of the government's programme to increase the participation of women in formal sector employment.

b.   In Mauritius, as described by Catherine Hein, the high level of demand for women workers in labour-intensive export industries is partly the result of the fact that the legal minimum wage is considerably lower for women than for men (Hein, 1982 and 1984). Another factor in Mauritius which contributes to the employers' preference for women workers is that they are considered easier to manage and control than men. Even if minimum wages were the same for men and women, it is likely that employers would continue to prefer women.

Results of the studies in Mauritus put into question the general assumption that an increase in women's work opportunities outside the home will necessarily influence marriage and child-bearing patterns (Hein, 1983). Women who had worked prior to marriage had not married any later than comparable women who had never worked. The timing of the births of the first and second children was also unrelated to current or prior employment. However, commitment to working as more than a temporary stage in life, rather than working per se, was found to have some relation to fertility behaviour.

c. and d. The two West African countries studied were both labour surplus economies where men have fared better than women in obtaining employment in the formal sector. Yet, in these societies, a large proportion of women have traditionally been active outside the home, often in petty trading. In both these studies, an institutional approach was adopted, with interviews of male and female employees as well as employers.

In Accra-Tema (Ghana), women's relatively low level of education was identified by Eugenia Date-Bah as an important barrier to their employment in the formal sector (Date-Bah, 1982). Nevertheless, it was noted that at a given level of education, men tend to occupy higher positions than women. The Nigerian study carried out in Ife by Lawrence Adeokum (Adeokun et al., 1984) found that women require a higher level of education than men to obtain formal sector employment. Other factors, apart from education, are thus clearly operating to the disadvantage of women.

Employers' attitudes and beliefs concerning women workers are limiting women's employment opportunities in both countries. In Ghana, employers consider women suitable for jobs involving activities such as cooking, nursing and secretarial work but not for jobs involving physical force, work with machines, or supervision. In Nigeria, women tend to be excluded from the modern catering industry, despite their high level of involvement in traditional catering services, partly because in larger-scale production there are more heavy jobs and more supervisory posts, for which women are considered unsuitable.

Both the Ghanaian and the Nigerian studies showed that employees, too, have definite ideas about the suitability of certain types of work for women, and that women are, in a sense, discriminating against themselves. Even for certain jobs where employers might consider women suitable, such as hotel and restaurant work, the derogatory image of women in such jobs makes women avoid them.

The relatively high level of fertility of women in both these societies is another factor influencing their availability for full-time salaried employment, and encouraging economic activity in the informal sector. Also, employers perceive the costs of employing women as high since they feel that maternity leave is costly both in terms of direct payments and in terms of indirect costs due to lost labour. Productivity is also felt by Ghanaian employers to fall somewhat during pregancy.

Discussion

The discussant, Mary Castro, stressed the need for more research on the use of women in labour-intensive export industries in developing countries. She felt this phenomenon should be discussed as part of the process of the internationalisation of capital.

She also pointed out the rather different beliefs of employers about women workers in the different countries. She suggested that the different logic of employers in the various settings must be understood as part of a whole context which includes the socio-economic structure of the country, and the employers' need to control the labour force as well as factors specific to the type of industry and enterprise.

In view of the findings concerning the disadvantaged position of women in the formal sector, the discussant felt that some action was required. She suggested that unions should be made more aware of the problems of women workers, as their actions could be important in promoting equality between men and women in employment. She also felt that ways of increasing women's participation in trade unions should be studied, as well as ways of stimulating the organisation of women workers, and that the ILO should be encouraged to take the lead in such studies and actions.

In the discussion which followed, participants emphasised how country-specific the various findings were. It was felt that such in-depth studies are important for understanding the dynamics of a given situation but cannot be generalised. The documenting and analysing of specific cases was also felt to be important as a guide to formulating appropriate policy measures.

It was noted by several participants that progress towards sexual equality in employment is more likely to occur in an economy with a labour shortage such as Cyprus than in one with a labour surplus such as Ghana. It was pointed out that women are more affected than men by the current widespread increases in unemployment. Additionally, unemployment among women tends to be under-estimated because women become discouraged and stop looking for work and are therefore no longer included in the unemployment statistics.

There was some discussion as to what "discrimination" really is. The ILO has various conventions and recommendations which give definitions, and which also indicate that equality is a major principle of the ILO. Participants agreed that it was important to understand discrimination as the result of the dynamic inter-play of institutional factors within a specific country rather than attributing it to characteristics of employers or employees.

IV. WOMEN'S ROLES, FERTILITY AND FAMILY PLANNING IN HIGH FERTILITY AREAS

1. Bangladesh, India, Ghana and Nigeria

Chairperson: Attiya Inayatullah

Papers:

a. Elahi, K. Maumood - "Family planning acceptance and women's programmes in Bangledeshi villages"

b. Oppong, Christine - "Case studies of women's roles, fertility and family planning in high fertility countries: Ghana and Nigeria" (reproduced in Section VIII)

c. Khan, M. Ejazuddin, Dastidar, S.K.G. and Bairathi, S. - "Women and health in India: A case study"

Discussants: Makhduma Nargis
                Ghazi Farooq

It is generally recognised that fertility rates are related to socio-economic and demographic factors such as mortality rates, educational levels, degree of urbanisation, and health and economic conditions, as well as customs and traditions. In particular, women's status, education, health and production activities are considered to be central determinants of fertility levels; unless there are changes in these areas, fertility rates are unlikely to decline in high fertility areas. The papers in this session concentrated on relevant findings on this subject from the ILO's research programme.

Papers

a.   Maumood Elahi's paper on Bangladeshi villages presented tentative observations arising from in-depth studies which form part of the ongoing UNFPA-funded, ILO-executed technical co-operation project on rural fertility and female employment. In 1977, the Government of Bangladsh re-oriented and organised its population programmes in a way which may be termed "beyond family planning". A multi-sectoral approach involving seven ministries was adopted in an effort to improve the health and education of women and children and raise the socio-economic status of women. Voluntary organisations and other social institutions were encouraged to participate, particularly in rural areas.

It was expected that such measures would lead to increased use of family planning and a long-term reduction in fertility. Observations from the Bangladeshi research are intended to give some indication of the impact of such programmes, although it is still too early to draw any firm conclusions about the changing status of rural women and their fertility.

In rural areas, employment (whether or not it is paid employment) does not seem to be related to lower levels of fertility. This is particularly true for women working in agri-culture or family-based cottage industries where women can keep their children with them while they work. Also, older children are valuable helpers with such work.

Education does seem to be related to a greater knowledge and use of family planning, although even among educated women only 10-13 per cent are currently practising family planning. It is important to note that family planning acceptance in the villages is still limited by irregularities in the distribution systems.

b.   The paper on Ghana and Nigeria by Christine Oppong presented four case studies on women's productive and repro-ductive roles. The paper pointed out that such small studies, at a minimum research cost, serve to underline the importance of putting into effect certain policies and programmes affecting women's employment and fertility. In addition they serve to throw more light on issues of social change in countries where national data sets are at present lacking, and, even where available, tell us little about the dynamic processes of change.

The first case study, by Patricia Lapido (forthcoming), involved a project to help Yoruba women in a maize storage co-operative. The results of the experiment suggested that access to loans and information through co-operative membership increased women's income, making them more able to cope with family demands and health needs, and also enhanced their desire to control their fertility. However, the adoption of family planning was hindered by lack of access to contraceptives at prices the women could afford and by continuing anxieties about infant mortality.

The second case study (Akuffo, forthcoming) looked at the reasons for the high drop-out rates of Ghanaian school girls and found pregnancy to be the main cause. This study underlines the need to include sex and family welfare education in adolescent schooling and vocational training projects.

The third case study (Oppong, 1983) was of Ghanaian men and investigated how aspects of their relationship with their wives, children and kin are related to reproductive goals and behaviour. It was found that they are less likely to want large families and more likely to use contraceptives consistently: (i) the more relationships in marriage are flexible and egalitarian; (ii) the more fathers assume individual responsibility for their offspring rather than indulging in traditional practices of having their children fostered by kin; and (iii) the more they have the same aspirations for their daughters' education as for that of their sons. In other words, factors concerning sexual equality in the domestic domain and individual responsibility are linked to demographic innovation. This study shows the importance of research on men's roles as parents and husbands if greater understanding is to be gained of fertility desires and the acceptance of family planning and also demonstrates the importance of including men as well as women in family life education programmes.

The fourth case study (Oppong and Abu, 1984) involved the analysis of sixty focused biographies of educated Ghanaian women varying in age, ethnic group, migrant status, and town of residence. Different types of employment and income generation, migration away from kin, and educational levels were seen to have multiple effects both upon behaviour and upon expectations. These changes can in turn be linked to a desire for fewer children of higher quality in terms of education and parental investment (maternal resources, time and interest). At the same time more systematic contraceptive use is associated with more child-care being done by the mother herself, looser links with kin, a more active individual role (with peers, friends), and an occupation which calls for longer hours of work away from home, thus causing perceptions of time strain and greater conflict between occupational and domestic activities.

c. In India, life expectancy for women is less than for men (52 years as compared to 55 years); the number of women per thousand men in the population has continued to decline throughout this century, and was 931 in 1981. The paper by Ejazuddin Khan et al. described how discrimination against women occurs in nutrition and health care from birth until death. The study is based on an ongoing project entitled "Changing Roles of Women and Its Impact on Their Demographic Behaviour" sponsored by the ILO. The data used in this paper were collected from a village in Uttar Pradesh by participant observation and other anthropological techniques over a period of about a year.

As babies, boys tend to be breastfed for longer than girls. When sick, boys are likely to be taken for medical treatment;

they tend to be taken at an earlier stage of the illness and for more expensive treatment. Boys constituted about three-quarters of the children brought for treatment at the Primary Health Centre in the study village. Of the 10 children who died in the village in 1981-82, seven were female; while all three boys had been taken to city hospitals for further treatment none of the girls had received such treatment.

Discrimination against female children was found to be greater among high castes than among low castes. One reason may be the dowry system prevalent among high caste Hindus which means that parents must pay a large sum of money on the marriage of their daughters. For low castes, the dowry is not a serious problem, and both women and girls work for cash earnings; in low caste families, girls are therefore less of an economic burden, and contribute earnings to the household until they are married.

As a wife living with her husband's family, a woman's health tends to be neglected. Cultural barriers such as purdah restrict their movements outside the home, including going to health care centres. It is common practice for male family members to visit the doctor in the place of the sick woman, narrating the woman's symptoms to the doctor. About two-thirds of the wives in the study could only consult a doctor if the husband agreed. Doctors admitted to exaggerating the illnesses of women to their husbands in order to ensure that the women were given care and medicine.

The diet of adult women is less substantial and less nutritious than that of men. It is felt by both men and women that the man, as "master of the house", should eat more. Furthermore, by tradition women take their meals only after serving all other members of the family and thus tend to get less.

The study concludes that although the health and diet of married women are neglected, they are still relatively privileged compared with other women because of their role in household work. Their medical treatment is inadequate but not totally lacking, as is the case of girls with many sisters or old women without any property.

Discussion

The discussant of the paper on Bangladesh, Makhduma Nargis, emphasised the importance of co-ordinating the efforts of various ministries and organisations. She also suggested a greater use of women's organisations and of trade unions (when the current ban on trade unions in Bangladesh is lifted).

Further research on the cultural barriers to family planning acceptance and on the impact of current programmes was also suggested, as was the need for research which would help to monitor problems in the implementation of field projects.

The discussant, Ghazi Farooq, emphasised the importance of linking research to policy formulation. He suggested that the

case study method does not produce data which can be generalised to a whole country and therefore from the point of view of
policy formulation cannot be a substitute for larger studies based
on representative samples. Such studies have their uses as a
supplementary method, however, for example for obtaining
insights into an underresearched group, for evaluating the
impact of interventions in a small community, and for studying
the problems of particular groups such as female-headed households.

He felt that policy research should be concerned with the
instruments of policy, giving some indication of the measures
which might be undertaken by the government in order to obtain
desired changes. The feasibility of such programmatic interventions should also be considered. He also felt that the
variables studied in policy-oriented research needed to have a
strong empirical relationship with the behaviour under consideration in order to justify any intervention by policy-makers.
Finally, he noted the need for policy-makers to be involved in
the research process, from the formulation of the research
questions to the evaluation of results.

In the general discussion, various issues mentioned in the
papers were highlighted as being important. One was teenage
pregnancy, which was mentioned as an area requiring research.
Participants also emphasised the persistence of high levels of
infant mortality as an important barrier to the reduction of
fertility in many developing countries, and the need for improved
health services. The perceived probability of a child dying was
mentioned as being important in fertility desires and behaviour,
as well as the desire for "high quality" children.

The general discussion subsequently focused on the relationship between research and policy. Some researchers expressed
concern that research may become too policy-oriented and
dominated by the interests of politicians and administrators. In
the case of fertility, the situation is very complex and much is
still unknown about its determinants. Basic research is still
needed at the country or even the regional level. Even in the
assessment of the demographic impact of specific projects, a
prior baseline survey is required in conjunction with subsequent
periodic evaluations. Researchers agreed on the need for
research which is of practical use, but emphasised the importance of basing applied research on more basic research.

The role of researchers vis-à-vis the utilisers of their
research was also discussed. It was suggested that the
researchers' role is to provide information on the relationships
between variables and what measures might be taken, but not to
decide what measures should be taken. The persons responsible
will normally have other factors outside the domain of the
researcher (political, budgetary, etc ` to take into account in
any decision.

The feeling was expressed that research findings are often
not utilised by those in responsible positions. One of the
reasons may be that researchers tend to write lengthy reports

filled with jargon, which senior officials do not have time to read. It was generally agreed that researchers must improve the presentation of their results, without oversimplifying the complexity of the process under consideration, and that there should be extensive interaction between researchers and policy-makers, from the planning stage until the presentation of the final report.

It was pointed out that governments are not the only users of research: depending on the content of the project, women's organisations, trade unions, employers' organisations, and community groups are also potential users, and should accordingly be involved in the research process.

2.   Uzbekistan (USSR), Colombia and Cuba

Chairperson: Attiya Inayatullah

Papers

a.   (i) Buriyera, Mamlakat - "A study of fertility in the Uzbek
SSR based on results of a socio-demographic survey"
(ii) Mulliadjanov, Iskhak - "Stability of the high birth rate
of Uzbekistan: An analytical overview"

b.   Castro, Mary - "Poor female heads of household and wives
in Bogota, Colombia"

c.   Farnos, Alfonso - "The demographic transition in Cuba:
Women's economic and social roles" (reproduced in Section
VIII)

d.   Alvarez-Lajonchere, Celestino - "Sex education in Cuba:
Roots and guidelines"

Discussants: Ghazi Farooq
Valentina Bodrova

In this session, the spotlight continued to be on high
fertility areas, this time in Latin America and in a republic of
the USSR. Cuba is no longer a high fertility area but was
included in this session because of the rapid decline in the birth
rate which has occurred over the last 15 years. One of the
main interests of this session was to try to understand why
fertility remains high in a developed area like Uzbekistan and
why it has declined rapidly in a developing country like Cuba.

Papers

a. Iskhak Mulliadjanov's paper on Uzbekistan stated that according to 1982 statistics the population of the republic is 16.6 million, representing 6.2 per cent of the population of the USSR. Over half (58 per cent) of the population lives in rural areas. The fertility rate in Uzbekistan is well above that of the USSR as a whole. The total fertility rate in 1979 was 5.1 (meaning a typical woman has about five children during her lifetime). The natural growth rate in 1981 was 2.77 per cent, as compared to 0.83 per cent for the USSR as a whole. Over the past 20 years (1960-80) the total number of new-born babies in the USSR dropped by 9 per cent, whereas in the Uzbek Republic it increased by 59 per cent.

Both birth rates and family size ideals vary considerably among different population groups within Uzbekistan. The two papers on Uzbekistan included various figures to show the much greater fertility of rural compared to urban women and of indigenous nationalities compared to those of European origin. The ideal number of children for women belonging to local ethnic groups is about 5-6. Socio-demographic surveys suggest, however, that family size ideals are slowly declining as women's educational standards increase and a higher proportion of women become skilled labourers.

Some of the reasons suggested for the high fertility rates in Uzbekistan are:

- The large proportion of the population which is rural.
- The stability of the family, with high marriage and low divorce rates. In 1981 there were only 1.4 divorces per thousand population.
- Lack of territorial mobility of the population: most people (77.7 per cent) remain in their birthplace.
- Continued existence of age-old traditions which attach a high value to motherhood and having many children.
- Lack of demographic awareness and negative attitudes to birth control.
- Survival of certain remnants of the feudal patriarchal structure of pre-revolutionary Uzbekistan.

b. Mary Castro's paper on Bogota, Colombia, discussed some of the results of a study which compared poor mothers living in a marital relationship with those not cohabiting with a male (female heads of households). The study included both a small survey of 98 mothers and 16 case studies in which successive interviews were conducted over three months. The proportion of women who are heads of households is increasing in Colombia with recent increases in the divorce rates as well as in the proportion of single women who are mothers.

The paper suggests that female-headed households are the "poorest of the poor". About half of the female heads of households received less than the official minimum salary, compared to a quarter of the husbands of the married women, although these groups were similar in age and education. (About 65 per cent of the wives who were working earned less than the minimum salary.) Women were more likely to be working in less protected occupations in the services sector, whereas men were more likely to be working in industry. In addition, the income of the male head of household was often supplemented by the earnings of his wife.

The majority of the female heads of households were the sole supporters of their children. On average, they had fewer children than the wives. Single mothers mostly explained their children as the result of their ignorance about sexual relations and pregnancy. Four-fifths of the female heads interviewed said they were not currently using contraception because they were not having regular sexual relations. They could thus be exposed to an unexpected pregnancy - and indeed unwanted pregancies among women living alone were high.

It is important to note the role of the husbands in the higher fertility of the wives. Having children is considered by wives as a way of pleasing and captivating their husband. Having a child is in general seen as a way of forcing men to live in a stable relationship.

This study thus provided some interesting insights into the condition of poor women in Bogota, and the mechanisms which influence their fertility. It also provided a number of research and policy-related conclusions. It pointed out the need for improved credit facilities for women; for women's organisations to be stimulated and strengthened; for sex education pro- grammes; for research results to be made available to local women's groups; and for improvement in the conceptualisation and measurement of the so-called "head of household" concept.

c. Alfonso Farnos' paper on Cuba documents the dramatic decline in fertility during the 1970s, from a gross reproduction rate of 1.80 in 1970 to 0.87 in 1980. At the same time, fertility has become more concentrated in the younger age groups: in 1970, for example, 48.2 per cent of fertility occurred in women aged 15-24 years as compared to 59.9 per cent in 1982 (see Farnos, Gonzalez and Hernandez, 1983).

The goals of the new Cuban society, as Farnos indicated, include increasing the integration of women into society, and in particular their participation in economic activity. In order to investigate the inter-relations between the reproductive behaviour of women and their economic participation, education, residence, etc., a research project was set up by the Cuban Women's Federation and the Demographic Research Centre of Havana University, which is now being finished with the help of the ILO. More than 3,000 women were interviewed in three selected areas of the country - one urban, one semi-urban and one rural.

The results of this survey indicate that fertility reduction has been fastest in rural areas; the rural/urban difference in fertility has therefore diminished significantly. This can be linked to the increasing use of contraception in rural areas. Abortion plays an important .part in controlling fertility, particularly in urban areas. One of the aims of sexual education in Cuba is to encourage the use of contraception as a means of birth control rather than abortion.

Overall, more than a quarter of the women interviewed had been married twice or more. The proportion of women who have been divorced is greater in urban areas, which may be related to the greater economic independence of women in these areas.

Fertility differences between women with different levels of education can still be observed, but they are not as great as in the past. Non-working women still tend to have more children than working women. This difference has become less in the last 10 years, but remains more marked in rural areas.

d. In his paper on Cuba, Celestino Alvarez-Lajonchere pointed out that the sharp decline in fertility during the 1970s was the result of complex changes within society and was never a goal of the government. Throughout this century, the fertility trend has been downwards, except for the first five years after the Revolution. The recent decline is found in all areas of the country, and is most rapid where fertility was highest.

The sex education programme in Cuba is part of a general plan of development. In principle, all citizens have the same rights not only before the law but also in social life. And when women are regarded as equal with men, sex education becomes a necessity. The Cuban Women's Federation (FMC) has been giving some sex education since 1960, and since the mid-1970s all government and mass organisations are obliged to implement a programme of sex education.

Although the main target of sex and family life education programmes is the younger generation, other age groups are also involved. One of the goals is in fact to improve relations between adolescents and adults. Another goal is to improve the situation of women by overcoming all forms of discrimination and exploitation, such as the double standard with regard to sex. For a sex education programme to be successful, Lajonchere indicated that it was necessary to have a strong commitment both at the programme and the political levels. The assistance of UNFPA and IPPF has also helped the Cuban Government in this area.

Discussion

In commenting on the decline of fertility in Cuba, the discussant, Ghazi Farooq, contrasted it with the declines which have been observed in other developing countries. In countries such as Pakistan, most of the small decline in fertility is due to an increase in the age of marriage. Yet in Cuba fertility is increasingly concentrated in the younger age groups and the marriage age may actually be decreasing.

Farooq suggested that the paper on female-headed households in Bogota was an example of how in-depth studies of specific disadvantaged groups could increase our understanding of the problems of that group and suggest measures to alleviate these problems.

In her comments on fertility trends in Cuba, the discussant Valentina Bodrova pointed out that the status of women had been changed by radical socio-economic transformations such as improved public health, the elimination of illiteracy, and increased participation of women in productive activity. In this context there are similarities between the dynamics of fertility decline in Cuba and in European socialist countries.

The discussant also noted that Uzbekistan, as part of the USSR, has also undergone radical socio-economic changes in the process of socialist transformation. Reclamation of new land and improved water supplies has expanded agricultural land and increased its productivity. With the assistance of other republics, there has been a rapid growth of employment in industry. The educational levels of the population, in particular of women, have become comparable to the rest of the USSR. Why then does the high fertility rate persist when such socio-economic factors usually seem to be related to declining fertility?

Bodrova emphasised certain factors:

- There have never been family planning programme campaigns in the republic, nor any other programmes aimed at limiting family size.

- Socio-economic measures have been designed to assist families with children. Education and medical facilities are free.

The discussant agreed with the authors of the papers that the socio-economic transformations currently under way in Uzbekistan were showing a tendency to reduce fertility because of their impact on the role of women.

The main topic in the open discussion was the factors involved in fertility decline. Various aspects of economic development may be involved, such as a decline in infant mortality, improved health facilities, increased education and employment of women, the declining proportion of the population working in agriculture, etc. Participants from high fertility developing countries wanted to know what lessons might be derived from the declines observed elsewhere, for example in Cuba. Since financial resources are limited they wanted to know what were the key factors responsible for reducing fertility; the solution of simply waiting for overall socio-economic development was considered impracticable, since it would take too long.

Some researchers considered that it was not possible to isolate particular factors, since complex relationships are involved in the determination of a demographic process. Many changes take place simultaneously, and it is impossible to say that any one change was the main factor in fertility change.

It was pointed out that the studies in this session could be interpreted as pointing to women's security as an important variable in fertility. Taking the case of the female heads of households in Bogota, the insecurity of their situation may encourage them to have children as a potential means of acquiring male support or eventually the support of children. In socialist countries, the economic security of women may have been a factor in the fertility decline. Again Uzbekistan is an interesting exception since the stability of the family is considered one of the reasons for high fertility there. More research on marital patterns and women's economic security and their relationship to fertility would be useful.

V. FERTILITY AND FEMALE EMPLOYMENT IN LOW FERTILITY SOCIALIST COUNTRIES

Chairperson: Valentina Bodrova

Papers:

a.   Bodrova, Valentina - "Employment of women in the socialist countries and demographic policy"

b.   Miltenyi, Karoly - "Fertility and female employment in Hungary"

c.   Pavlik, Zdenek - "Fertility and female employment in Czechoslovakia"

d.   Turchaninova, Svetlana - "The female employment situation in the Soviet Union" (reproduced in Section VIII)

e.   Farnos, Alsonso and Gonzalez Quinones, F. - "Fertility and female employment in Cuba"

f.   Mikhailova, Pavlina - "Fertility and female employment in Bulgaria"

Discussants: Eva Mueller
                Zdenek Pavlic

Many centrally planned socialist countries have low birth rates and high female labour force participation rates. In these countries, a concentrated effort has been made to help women combine motherhood with working outside the home by means of measures such as extended paid maternity leave, free creches, school canteens, etc. The aim of such measures is to promote the social equality of women and men, both at work and in society generally, and also to protect pregnant women and children. The experience of these countries is thus very relevant to a discussion of female employment and fertility. Most of the papers given in this session are based on detailed studies which will be published in a forthcoming book edited by Bodrova and Anker, Working women in socialist countries: The fertility connection.

Papers

     a. Valentina Bodrova described the growth of female employ-. ment in the national economies of socialist countries since the Second World War. She also pointed out that the proportion of working women in skilled or highly skilled occupations has been growing under the impact of scientific and technological progress. However, at present the skill level of female personnel is still lower than what is potentially possible and desirable because the problems of combining work outside the home with maternal and domestic responsibilities have not been adequately taken into account.

     Bodrova cited evidence from a time budget survey of working women in the USSR, which showed that after the birth of the first child, the amount of time spent sleeping is reduced by three hours per week. Sociological research also shows that the professional growth of women is often checked if they have two or more children.

     One of the primary aims of social and demographic policy in the socialist countries is to improve the working and living conditions of working mothers. The labour legislation of European socialist countries accordingly prohibits women from working in jobs which may damage their health such as under-ground work, or work involving the handling of dangerous chemicals or exposure to radiation. Special legislation protects pregnant women and mothers of babies from assignment to night work, overtime, and business trips.

     In all European socialist countries women are granted long periods of maternity leave, paid out of social security funds, ranging from 112 days in Poland and Rumania to 182 days in Czechoslovakia and the German Democratic Republic. After paid maternity leave, additional partially paid leave to care for small children is granted in Bulgaria, Hungary, the German Democratic Republic and Czechoslovakia. Other provisions to assist working mothers that have been introduced in the various socialist countries of Europe include time off for breastfeeding, paid leave to care for a sick child, reduced working hours, and prolonged annual leave.

     b. Karoly Miltenyi discussed the reasons for the fertility decline in Hungary. The decrease in fertility was especially rapid after the Second World War, though interspersed with temporary increases caused partly by demographic factors (such as age structure) and partly by the mostly short-term effects of certain population policy measures (see Barta, Klinger, Miltenyi and Vukovich, 1983 and 1984).

     The basic causes of the fertility decline in Hungary can be summarised as follows:

     (i)   Increasing economic activity of women. Women now represent about 45 per cent of the labour force; an increasing proportion of women are employed, especially in the young age groups. Since the fertility of active women has traditionally been lower than that of non-active women, this has had the effect of lowering the overall level of fertility.

(ii)   Increasing educational attainment of women. The increasing proportion of women with secondary or tertiary level education (whose fertility is relatively low) has helped to decrease overall fertility, in spite of the fact that within given educational categories the fertility level has remained more or less constant.

(iii)   Structural changes in the national economy and concomitant social mobility. Fertility has always been highest among peasants and lowest among non-manual workers, with manual workers in between. Although differences in the fertility of the different social strata have decreased over time, they still continue to exist. Rapid social mobility from agricultural to non-agricultural occupations and from manual to non-manual work has thus helped to accelerate the decline in fertility.

(iv)   Urbanisation and migration. Couples moving from villages to towns generally adopt the urban lower fertility pattern: sometimes the urban immigrant's fertility may be even lower than that of the original urban population.

(v)   Economic considerations. In Hungary, over 9 per cent of the net national product in 1980 was spent on social benefits and assistance related to children, i.e. family allowance, child-care allowance, institutional care, free education, etc. In spite of all this, the standard of living in a household is strongly influenced by the number of dependent children. Also housing conditions, especially the inhabitant/room ratio, are correlated with the size of the family.

(vi)   Knowledge and availability of birth control methods. The period 1956-73 was characterised by a high ratio of induced abortions to births, as permission for abortion was granted on request. In 1973 some restrictions were introduced because of the unfavourable effects on health of repeated abortions. At the same time, general and pre-marriage consultation on contraception was started, and access to modern contraceptives, including the pill, was facilitated. The proportion of contraceptive users then increased rapidly, the pill and the IUD becoming the main methods.

(vii)   Rising divorce rate and increase in the number of one-parent families. The stability of a marriage greatly affects the family size. Although, in the case of remarrying females, divorce and remarriage do not always mean smaller completed fertility, in recent years high divorce rates have been accompanied by decreasing rates of remarriage. The proportion of one-parent families - usually mother and child or children - has thus increased.

To sum up, almost all aspects of socio-economic development and the concomitant structural changes have had the effect of lowering fertility. Partial or ad hoc population policy measures may have had the effect of temporarily raising the birth rate; however, they could not reverse the generally decreasing trend of fertility.

c. In his paper, Zdenek Pavlik noted that Czechoslovakia has traditionally had a high level of economic activity among women, and this increased further in the last two census periods (1961-70, 1970-80). In the last census period, the highest increase was in the 25-34 age group, when women are still in the main child-bearing period.

The increase in the number of economically active women since 1961 can be explained by two factors: the fall in the fertility level in the 1960s and the population policy measures introduced in the 1970s. The aim of these measures was to overcome conflicts between maternal duties and work (women on maternity leave are considered as economically active in Czecho-slovakia). It is not possible to judge which factor was more important.

Economically active women in Czechoslovakia have always had fewer children on average than women who did not work. However, the type of economic activity is more important for fertility than whether the women works or not. Employees (i.e. non-manual workers) have the lowest level of fertility and agricultural workers the highest. Diffferences between social groups are nevertheless declining. There is also a relationship between a woman's educational level and her family size, but this, too, is becoming less important.

Two other points can be discussed in connection with female employment and fertility in Czechoslovakia: the time use of working women and the standard of living of families with children. The available data concerning the time use of women and men has shown that for economically active women the work they do at home takes up only a slightly smaller amount of time than the work outside the home; they have at home the second shift. Women therefore have significantly less free time than men. Women work on average 25.2 hours a week at home, and men 14.5 hours. Only in younger families do men participate to any greater extent in the work at home. In many families a grandmother represents a considerable help to a woman working outside the home. It is interesting that time spent on house-work and child-care did not depend on the number of children.

- 44 -

In spite of a rising standard of living, income differences among households with different numbers of children, or no children, are still pronounced. A study in 1975 showed that the income per person in households with four children was only half that of childless families. The largest jump is probably that from one to two child families, i.e. 16 points (childless family = 100). It is likely that the policy measures aimed at increasing fertility in Czechoslovakia in the 1970s affected mostly the birth of second children.

Pavlik's view is that fertility and female employment are undoubtedly inter-connected, but through many other social institutions. Conclusions cannot therefore be unequivocal, and further research needs to be directed to the problems of families, their stability, and their position in society, in the context of overall economic and social reproduction.

d. In the Soviet Union, as described by Svetlana Turchaninova, consistent efforts have been made to achieve a genuine social and economic equality between women and men and, more specifically, to create satisfactory conditions for women to combine their two social functions as creators of material and cultural wealth and as mothers and educators of the younger generation. These conditions include various social benefits, particular consideration of working women's occupational safety and health, the steady improvement of working conditions, vocational training and retraining opportunities, and increasing government aid to the family.

In the 1970s, the rate of economic participation of women of productive age was 90-93 per cent, 7.5 per cent of them being engaged in full-time studies. Since 1970, the share of women in the national labour force has stood at a national average of 51 per cent, not going below 40 per cent in any individual constituent republic. Women at work constitute 51 per cent of all industrial workers and office employees, 54 per cent of collective farmers, 55 per cent of specialists, 47 per cent of research workers, 29 per cent of construction workers, 63 per cent of administrative workers, 73 per cent of workers in education and recreation, 82 per cent of workers in health, physical recreation and social security, and 83 per cent of workers in commerce and public catering.

Turchaninova indicated that a high rate of female labour force participation is not in itself a sufficient test of rational female labour force utilisation unless it is accompanied by fertility and reproduction patterns that meet the needs of social development. In other words, whatever the social and economic benefits of increased participation in the national economy by women, it is also necessary to consider its possible effects on population trends.

Among the many socio-economic and psychological causes of the declining birth rate in the Soviet Union, the high level of female labour force participation is one of the more important. The greatest drop in the birth rate was registered during the

1960s because it was during that decade that large numbers of women left the home economy and the family holding to participate in social production.

The paper added that participation of some women of working age in the home economy is an important element in a rational female employment pattern - not that they should be excluded from the national economy once and for all but rather than they should leave productive work temporarily to give birth and raise children. Soviet studies show that the average working woman in the 1960s participated in social production for an average of 28.7 years as compared to 33.5 years in the 1970s.

e.   The paper by Alfonso Farnos on Cuba noted that the economic participation of women has increased considerably since the Revolution in 1957. According to the 1953 census, women accounted for only 17 per cent of the economically active population; in 1970, this proportion was 23.8 per cent, and in 1981 it had reached 31.3 per cent. The results of the sample surveys mentioned in the previous paper on Cuba (see Section IV) permit an in-depth study of the relationship between women's employment and fertility. A comparison of the occupational status of employed mothers with that of their daughters demonstrates a pronounced change in women's occupational patterns.

The proportion of women employed in low-income occupations is declining and the number of women employed as domestic servants has dropped to zero. In 1958 job opportunities for women were mostly confined to domestic service and farming, while at the present time over 50 per cent of all employed women work in such sectors as public health or as technical personnel in the manufacturing and mining industries. These trends in the educational and employment patterns of women helped to bring about a rapid decline in the fertility rate. It is noteworthy that the difference in the total fertility rate between urban and rural areas was less than that between employed (1.63) women and non-working women (2.51).

Women's occupational group was also related to their fertility. Women who were agricultural or manual workers had a higher fertility rate than administrative personnel, personnel in service industries, technicians, and professionals, although this difference was more marked in rural areas than in urban or semi-urban areas.

The paper concludes that a complex set of factors is influencing fertility trends but that the most important are the qualitative changes in women's economic role in society and in the family, in terms of their level and type of involvement in the national economy.

f. The paper on Bulgaria, presented by Pavlina Mikhailova pointed out that women's labour force participation rates are now about the same as those of men; in 1979 women constituted 49 per cent of economically active persons. The increase in female labour force participation is the logical result of the economic and social progress of the country, and of state policies aimed at increasing women's participation in economic, social and cultural life. It is interesting to note that for the period 1965-75 almost the entire increase in the economically active population was due to the increase in the number of active women.

In 1975, as far as the occupations of men and women are concerned, there was an equal, or almost equal, distribution of men and women amongst manual workers, co-operative peasants, and non-manual worker specialists. Amongst managers and non-manual worker specialists with university education, men still predominated, whereas women were predominant among co-operative craftsmen.

A study of persons in managerial positions shows that the proportion of women in managerial positions does not correspond to the proportion of women in the economically active population of the country, nor to their level of education or professional training. In Mikhailova's opinion, this is because of deeply rooted stereotypes as to the social qualities of women - stereotypes which suggest that womanliness is incompatible with the qualities of a manager. It is expected, however, that these stereotypes will change in time.

From 1951 onwards, the crude birth rate in Bulgaria has generally shown a declining trend, from 25.2 per thousand in 1952 to 14.5 in 1980. Various policy measures to stimulate the birth rate did result in increases just after their implementation, but these effects were short-lived. Between 1965 and 1975, the average number of live-born children per married woman declined from 2.01 to 1.87, and the proportion of women with three or more children also declined. The amount of time between the birth of the first and second child increased.

Education exerts a substantial influence on changes in the reproductive behaviour of contemporary Bulgarian women, higher levels of education being associated with a smaller number of children. The differences diminished between 1965 and 1975, however, since educated women were having slightly more children than before. Nevertheless, given that the proportion of married women at higher educational levels increased over the period, the overall average number of live-born children decreased.

Differences in the number of children between economically active and non-active women are not all that great. In any case, almost all women work. Fertility differences are related, rather, to the nature of women's employment and their level of professional attainment.

Time use data provides some interesting information on how the number of children affects women's work load in the home. With each additional child (until the fourth) the time the mother spends on housework and child-care increases, the increase being particularly great between the first and second child. In general, the degree of sharing of housework between men and women is minimal. It is possible that this household situation is also a factor in lowering fertility.

Discussion

The discussant, Eva Mueller, remarked that the measures taken by governments in Eastern Europe to help women reconcile their productive and reproductive roles were striking. One would have expected that such measures would increase fertility, yet the papers suggest that their main influence has been on the timing of births rather than on completed fertility. If so, then the causes of low fertility in Eastern Europe must lie elsewhere, perhaps in the common cultural values shared by both Eastern and Western Europe. Other factors which may be partially responsible for the low fertility rate in Eastern Europe are increasing consumerism and the striving for a higher standard of living, which are also thought to be influential in Western Europe and North America. This possibility is suggested by statistics in papers that show the variation in the standard of living of households as a function of the number of children.

Statistics showing differences in fertility levels between women who work outside the home and those who do not are difficult to interpret, Mueller felt. Is activity status the cause or the result of the fertility level? In addition, activity status at any point in time may be temporary. It is important to use statistics with a longer time reference, such as the number of years women have been in the labour force, or the number of years they intend to stay in it.

The two papers which report time use data (those on Czechoslovakia and Bulgaria) report rather different effects on women's work in the home of increasing numbers of children. As Mueller pointed out, such differences are very surprising, and may in fact be due to different methods of collecting data, for example the scoring procedure used when more than one activity is carried out at the same time.

The discussant also raised the question of the labour force participation of older women, and how this might affect their daughters' ability to work once they had children.

The discussant concluded that it was difficult to say which were the main reasons for low fertility in the countries discussed in this session. While women's level of education was clearly an important factor, which should be noted by less developed countries, the other lessons were less clear.

The discussant Zdenek Pavlik pointed out that all the papers in this session dealt with the historical-demographic factors influencing demographic change, but felt that it was difficult to isolate any particular variable as crucial. The effect on fertility of the increasing educational levels of women, for example, cannot really be isolated from the effects of other social changes which were occurring simultaneously.

An understanding of the demographic revolution is important for all countries, but the effect of a change such as the increased labour force participation of women will depend on the fertility level of the particular country, the discussant felt. Also, once once the demographic revolution is over in a country, fertility may be influenced by a rather different set of factors. New patterns can be seen emerging in Eastern Europe, and various new issues have arisen:

(i)   Time use data show that women, despite their work outside the home, still spend much more time on housework and child-care than men.   What are the implications of this situation for fertility?

(ii)   Fertility decline tends to be accompanied by a narrowing of differences in fertility between occupational, educational and social groups. Will this homogenisation process continue, or will some differences persist?

The work patterns and socio-economic aspirations of the populations in Eastern Europe may not be consistent with the pro-natalist population policies of the governments.   It is important that such population policies should form an integral part of social policy, in order to create conditions in which families can have the number of children desired without lowering their standard of living.

In considering the effect of fertility levels on women's position in the labour market, the discussant pointed out that sexual equality in the labour market depends on equality in the home and the sharing of household tasks.   In some cases, measures such as extended child-care leave may discourage sharing in the home; the husband may work longer hours to compensate for the decline in family income while the wife concentrates on housework and child-care.

In the open discussion, it was emphasised that in the USSR and Eastern Europe demographic policy is seen as part of social policy.   The aim is to change the demographic parameters to make it easier for women to work outside the home, and also to improve the standard of living of the people.   Family size ideals are difficult to change, but measures can at least be taken to help those who want two or three children to realise their ideal. It was also pointed out that the policies aimed at increasing the compatibility of work and child-care may have a negative effect on male-female equality in the workplace.   Since women continue to take on most of the burden of the household work and the rearing of children, the availability of extended maternity (or paternity) and child-care leave is taken advantage of only by the women.   These extended breaks in service in turn adversely affect women's long-term job prospects.

Participants disagreed on whether it was possible to separate out and rank the factors responsible for declining fertility in any particular context.   Women's level of education was acknowledged to be important, but there was disagreement as to whether it was important in its own right or as part of a more general development process.

From the point of view of developing countries which are trying to reduce fertility, general socio-economic development is a solution which is considered to be beyond their current financial means and too slow in its impact on fertility. On the other hand, the experience of the socialist countries in trying to influence fertility through policy measures was not considerd very encouraging for developing countries. Despite the substantial benefits given to children and mothers, long-term fertility trends do not seem to have been greatly affected by these measures. This suggests that the factors underlying fertility patterns are strongly entrenched in the culture and not easily influenced by incentive schemes.

In general, it was agreed that in all countries it was important to see fertility goals as part of the more general goal of improving the living conditions of the population and allowing women to take part in economic and social life on an equal footing with men.

VI. INFORMATION FOR POLICY FORMULATION: UTILISATION OF RESEARCH FOR WOMEN'S AND POPULATION ISSUES

1. Agency and trade union perspectives

Chairperson: Christine Oppong

Papers:

a.   Doctor, Kailas - "UNFPA programme"

b.   Smirnova, Raissa - "ILO development of research on women workers' questions"

c.   Doctor, Kailas - "Women's issues from the perspective of the ILO's population programme"

d.   Mueller, Eva - "Research for policy formulation in high fertility developing countries"

e.   Turchaninova, Svetlana Ya - "Soviet trade union activities to improve the position of working women"

f.   Nargis, Makhduma - "Trade union perspective on utilisation of research for women's and population issues: Bangladesh"

g.   Alagawadi, Usha - "Trade union perspective on the utilisation of research: India"

Discussants: Attiya Inayatullah
                Evros Demetriades

Papers

Kailas Doctor spoke on behalf of UNFPA, since representatives of this organisation were unable to attend the seminar.

He noted that UNFPA is the leading organisation for funding in the area of population activities; international population assistance amounts to approximately $700 million per year, out of which UNFPA's share is around $130 million. About 70 per cent of the UNFPA budget is allocated to family planning and related information and communication projects, and the remaining 30 per cent to data collection, censuses, and population and development activities. Research should have a practical orientation, and for global research projects such as those at the ILO, priority needs to be given to the development of appropriate research tools for eventual use by nationals interested in policy research.

After the World Conference for the UN Decade for Women (Mexico, 1975), UNFPA set up a unit on women's issues and funds were made available for projects concentrating on women and fertility, such as the one at the ILO which is the focus of this seminar. However, with the recent financial crisis at UNFPA, family planning projects have been given priority for the limited funds available. It is felt at UNFPA that women's projects should be integrated into other development projects and not be kept separate. In the future, it is hoped that UNFPA will take a broader perspective on population and family planning issues taking into account women's activities in the family, community, economy and society, and their demographic aspects.

b. Raissa Smirnova, Chief of the ILO Office for Women Workers' Questions, stated that since 1975 a comprehensive programme of activities has evolved within the ILO on women workers' questions such as international standard setting, discrimination and promotion of equality in employment, population, technology, rural women, and female-headed households.

Programmes and budgets have focused on providing better data on the economic and social contribution of women to the economy and to society. Activities include updating of statistical information, of legislative surveys (including maternity protection), research studies, and publications such as the ILO news bulletin Women at Work in order to disseminate recent research findings and obtain better insights on the links between women's issues and socio-economic structures.

The common objective of the above activities is to describe in broad terms the evolution of the employment situation of women workers (depending on the availability of statistics) and to examine the impact on women of certain major developments since 1975. The background paper "Women and development - An assessment of the situation", which the Office for Women Workers' Questions has submitted to the seminar, shows that the global struggle for equality of opportunity and treatment for men and women workers is not yet won.

ILO figures show that in 1950 women formed 31.3 per cent of the global labour force while in 1975 they represented 35 per cent. According to ILO estimates, the increasing trend will not continue during the coming decades. In 1980 women represented only 34.8 per cent of the total labour force, an actual decline since 1975. This quasi-stagnation is expected to continue throughout the remainder of this century.

It is important to note that the above figures severely under-represent the real extent of women's work. It is well known that women in many parts of the world work long hours in agriculture, animal husbandry, household work, and the production of goods and services for the informal sector, without being counted among the economically active population. This again has serious consequences for the evaluation of women's work, for national policy formulation, and for development planning in general.

The figures nevertheless indicate clearly that in the course of the last few decades women have been drawn into the labour market in large numbers and that the contribution of women to their country's economic and social progress is far from marginal. In other words, women are an integral part of the production of goods and services. The well-being of women workers is therefore not a question to the relegated to the social welfare debate, but a question that touches the core of the entire production process, and which has important policy implications.

Discriminatory attitudes, which consider women as a secondary labour force, to be called upon in the hour of need and dismissed in times of unemployment, still prevail in many circles. To implement and enforce the legal right to work and give women equality of access to employment would need action at all levels, national and international, from guarantees in the constitution to altering legislation and translating it into practice. The task is not simply to proclaim the right of women to work but also to ensure it by the whole system of economic and political organisation of society.

As we move to the end of the UN Decade for Women: Equality, Development and Peace, we shall have to consider seriously once again the deeper roots of the economic and social phenomena that so greatly affect women workers and review and re-evaluate the World Plan of Action (1975) and the Programme of Action (1980). In 1985, during the Third UN World Conference on Women scheduled to be held in Nairobi, there will be another grand opportunity to look at global issues concerning women.

c. Kailas Doctor, Chief of the ILO's Population and Labour Policies branch, discussed the work of this branch, with particular reference to women.

The ILO's Population and Labour Policies Programme, most of which is financed by the United Nations Fund for Population Activities, consists of three components:

(i)   Family welfare education and family planning in work settings.

(ii)   Global research to develop new approaches to the interactions between demographic variables and employment factors, and new methods of measuring and analysing these interactions.

(iii)   Policy and research work of an operational nature to integrate population factors into human resources development policies and planning.

The research project "Women's Roles and Demographic Change" has various policy implications. A major focus is the measurement of the female labour force and related methodological issues. Insights gained should, at the very least, help to refine or adjust data on women's labour force participation from conventional sources such as population censuses and labour force surveys. Questions are being developed which may lend themselves to direct operational use in standard labour force surveys; they may therefore help to increase the precision of the primary data. A related effort is to estimate the value of unpaid work in the household. Proper recognition of women as productive workers and of the value of the work they do in the home should have the effect, at the national and global levels, of raising the status of women.

Studies on urban women workers lend themselves more readily to analysis and policy action since a sizeable number of urban women workers are likely to be in the formal sector and therefore within the purview of labour and development policy measures and relevant action by unions and managements.

The problems of women in reconciling their roles as mother and worker is a theme which runs through all the ILO research under this project - in both low fertility and high fertility countries. In high fertility countries, consciousness of this conflict may spur women towards acceptance of family planning, and perhaps encourage smaller families in the long term. The specific components of development policies and programmes - especially at the community and local levels - which reinforce the efforts being made to promote family planning practices and thus to reduce fertility, need to be identified. Research work which throws light on these issues is of great value for policy and programme purposes in the field of population and family planning.

The ILO was the executing agency of several UNFPA-funded technical co-operation projects in the Middle East and Asian countries (including Cyprus, Egypt, PDRY, Iraq, Jordan, Sudan and Bangladesh) which were designed, among other things, to help improve the economic position of women in terms of increasing female labour force participation, reducing labour market segmentation and discrimination against women, etc., and to encourage desired changes in the number of children people have. Most countries where these projects were operational are keen to increase the level of women's economic activity, but as far as national population policies are concerned there is a marked variation.

The full potential of interaction between the research project and policy-making activities on related themes is as yet only partially drawn upon. Much more remains to be done. The new thrust at the ILO will be towards understanding the development process at the community level and its impact on fertility. Results from empirical studies seeking to identify critical change agents will be used as a basis for policy formulation and the evaluation of policy implementation.

d. In her paper, Eva Mueller described how research may be used to stimulate interest in population and women's issues and can provide information which assists policy design and implementation.

The use of research to stimulate interest in population policy is illustrated by a large project sponsored by the US Agency for International Development (USAID). Under a programme called "Rapid" computer-assisted presentations of the economic and social consequences of demographic change for a particular country can be given. The main advantage of displaying these relationships in colour on a computer screen (instead of showing charts or slides) is that it allows for an interactive presentation. This means that experiments with the model, based, for example, on alternative assumptions about the values of exogenous variables on key parameters, can be part of the presentation. Most of the questions raised by the audience can be answered on the spot.

The computer could, for example, be programmed to project over a period of 10-25 years the effect of different rates of population growth in Rwanda on the size of the school age population, the number of new school teachers needed, the number of new school buildings needed and their cost, and the size of the educational budget required for various levels of school attendance. If the audience were interested, the computer could quickly tell them how much the educational budget could be reduced if the crude birth rate were 2.5 per cent instead of 3 per cent, or if the schooling requirements were cut back by a year, or if the teacher/student ratio were lowered, and so on.

The objective of Rapid is thus to communicate research findings in a way which makes the material understandable to audiences which are not composed of economists, or demographers, or statisticians. The importance of presenting research findings in a simplified way which makes them interesting and accessible to non-specialists and which stimulates discussion is often under-estimated or entirely overlooked.

Of course, popular presentations have inherent limitations in that the audience may be suspicious of over-simplifications. The Rapid presentations have had a mixed reception in developing countries. In some countries they have been rejected as obvious propaganda in favour of family planning, in others they have been received with great interest.

In a sense, the best possible outcome of a Rapid presentation is a decision by the government to create its own version of the model, collect data for it, and publicise its own results. For the ultimate objective of Rapid is to impart techniques of analysis which, if properly assimilated, will allow governments to take full account of potential economic-demographic interactions in their planning process.

Concerning the relationship between research and policy measures, Mueller noted that in a number of projects which attempted to increase women's involvement in activities outside the home, especially economic activities, there has been little research to evaluate their demographic impact. More generally, good studies of demographic impact are rare. She expressed the hope that seminar participants from developing countries who are, or will be, involved in development projects which attempt to improve the status of women, will see to it that data are collected which will throw light on the linkages between various changes in women's status and changes in family size, child mortality, migration, age at marriage, and the like.

e. Svetlana Turchaninova described how the Soviet trade unions take an active part in the implementation of government policy, with the aim of expanding Soviet women's opportunities in all spheres of economic and social life. Women's commissions function in all union bodies. These commissions work for improvements in the position of employed women; they discuss problems and draw up proposals for long-term plans for the expansion of union activities to improve women's working and living conditions, and mother and child welfare.

Since 1978 each collective agreement has included a special section on the improvement of conditions for women workers and assistance in child-care; these set out measures to be taken to raise the skills of women workers and to provide better services, health care, and opportunities for rest and recreation, both for the female employees and for their families, especially children. At the proposal of the AUCCTU (All Union Central Council of Trade Unions), factory and other industrial executives are now required to submit to the government regular progress reports on collective agreements. The AUCCTU commission will then have at its disposal enough data to monitor how the collective agreements are being implemented in various regions and sectors of the economy in order to take prompt corrective action, if required.

In their activities the trade unions and their commissions draw on the recommendations of research centres. At present nearly 70 research groups (including the labour research institute in Ivanvo - one of the six labour protection research institutes run by the AUCCTU) are involved in studies of the female labour force and related problems.

These research centres are concerned with problems of female workers that call for well-balanced and speedy solutions.

Their programmes address such issues as the development of the family, possibilities for combining employment and motherhood, and the rational use of female labour. To take some examples, the evaluation of socio-economic and biomedical criteria to assess the efficiency of female labour in different industries and occupations provided the basis for some recommendations. An examination of the reasons for the skills of women workers in some industries being inferior to those of male workers led to the development of guidelines for the improvement of training programmes for the female labour force. Studies of the health of pregnant women in conditions that may be hazardous to their health helped elaborate appropriate recommendations on their employment.

     f. The union representative from Bangladesh, Makhduma Nargis, first described some of the realities in Bangladesh: crude birth rate, 46 per thousand; infant mortality, 140 per thousand live births; acres of land per person, 0.55. Landless labourers constitute 55 per cent of all agricultural labourers, and 85 per cent of the total population lives below the poverty line. Growing pauperisation of the rural masses is apparent. Social and religious prejudices coupled with existing production relationships relegate women to a low status in the community. Population and socio-economic developmental issues are thus interrelated, and neither can be approached in isolation. There has to be a growing realisation that the population explosion is a multi-dimensional problem affecting the social, economic and health conditions of the people and requires a multi-faceted effort to solve it.

Nargis emphasised the inadequacy of current data on women's labour force participation in Bangladesh. According to the 1974 census, 2.5 per cent of women aged 10 years or above participate in the labour force; among 15.48 million agricultural labour force workers, only 3.48 per cent (0.61 million) are women. This picture is totally misleading, however. The activities of rural women, although mostly unpaid, are critical to the processing of food grains, the preservation and storage of seeds, and the production of food for the family - rearing poultry and livestock, and growing vegetables. In weaving and fishing communities women contribute substantially spinning thread for handlooms and making fishing nets. One significant aspect of all these activities should be pointed out: they can be carried out in the privacy of the home without violating the purdah system. Studies have observed that in Bangladesh rural women spend 12-14 hours daily in productive work, as opposed to the 10-11 hours spend by men.

The actual economic activities of rural women are not well documented in Bangladesh, nor is their possible impact on population issues. Moreover, the data presently available from sample surveys are often collected by expatriate organisations, by males, or by urban-educated females without proper insight into rural society. The paper suggested that unless basic and inherent weaknesses in information-gathering systems are corrected, they will continue to act as an impediment to any fruitful research work.

g. The union representative from India, Usha Alagawadi, stated that research on women's questions and the insights gained can help the unions in their struggle against sex discrimination in employment, and help to clarify many of the misconceptions regarding women's positions, capabilities, roles, etc. Armed with research results, it may be possible for unions to make enough impact on policy-makers to bring about the necessary changes at the governmental level. In this way links can be established between researchers, trade unions and policy framers.

Alagawa felt that the population problem needed to be viewed in the overall context of socio-economic relationships. What developing countries urgently need is a proper economic policy aimed at restructuring society and speeding up development, while ensuring an equitable distribution of resources. Higher standards of living bring about a fall in birth rates. Raising the social status of women and implementing an intelligent employment policy would go further in controlling population growth than compulsory family planning measures.

Discussion

The discussant Attiya Inayatullah made a number of comments concerning research on women and demography and its utilisation. She regretted that the research conducted by various UN agencies was mainly unco-ordinated. Existing data is not fully utilised and the analyses done tend to be weak because they stay at the descriptive level rather than looking at dynamic relations between variables, which is what is really important for policy decisions.

The discussant emphasised the mutual benefit which would be derived from greater contact between planners and researchers. For example, planners often lack regular and reliable data for forecasting the labour force and employment opportunities. The ILO can help in this respect, but through a dialogue with governments not by imposing international research tools. She also stressed the need for effective dissemination of research results; presentations should be short, concise, and understandable. Better dissemination might in certain cases increase the political will to take action and help break the inertia of bureaucracy.

In the context of large countries such as Pakistan, it is important that research be decentralised because of the great regional differences which exist. Planning should take place at the local level; qualitative micro-studies are of tremendous value in this context. Development should start at the grass-roots level with the full involvement of the people. Development projects should take an integrated, holistic approach and have a built-in monitoring system in which local people participate.

As concerns the programme Rapid mentioned by Mueller, which has been used in Pakistan, one problem arose. The age structure of a population with a high proportion of young people made it difficult to see any quick results from population measures. Use of such a computer could thus lead to a certain discouragement.

The discussant Evros Demetriades emphasised the need for wider dissemination of research results to all potential users. They will then become aware of the existence of information relevant to their work and be in a position to exchange ideas with researchers. In this way, the content of research is likely to improve. It is also important that research results should be disseminated quickly.

Both population growth and under-estimation of women's economic contribution are multi-dimensional, complex issues. But priorities and specific objectives must be set, taking into account the cost-benefit aspect. The tendency to incorporate too many topics into an enquiry should be avoided, as this reduces the quality of the replies and increases costs.

According to Demetriades, international organisations such as the ILO have a key role to play in the development of the infrastructure for carrying out research, training personnel, and disseminating information. He also stressed that if research is to be useful to trade unions there needs to be a dialogue between researchers and trade unions; flexible working hours, labour market discrimination, and international standard setting are some of the research topics which should be of interest to trade unions.

The participants in the open discussion stressed the need for comprehensive research on population issues. To concentrate on family planning was considered too narrow an approach to such a complex issue, about which so little is known. There was general agreement that simple KAP (knowledge, attitude and practice) surveys of family size and family planning tend to be misleading, since they ignore the more complex issues.

The importance of involving various types of organisations apart from governments in the research process was also emphasised. Several participants stressed the need for research to involve grass roots, local and regional organisations so as to increase the quality of the research and the people's awareness of it. Trade unions, where they exist, can also play an important role, as described in the paper on the USSR.

In general, it was felt that researchers need to give more attention to the dissemination of information and make sure that it reaches all those concerned, including those who were the objects of the research.

It was pointed out that global research may not be immediately translatable into policy recommendations. Such recommendations can normally be made only at the national level. However, global research is important for developing the frame-work and tools for research at the national, regional, or community level. A number of participants expressed regret that international funding agencies concerned with population issues such as UNFPA were becoming increasingly restrictive in the funding of population-related research - especially in the light of the numerous failures of narrowly based family planning programmes all over the world.

2.   Government perspective

Chairperson: Kailas Doctor

Papers:

a.   Inayatullah, Attiya   Pakistan (reproduced in
                                     Section VIII)

b.   Chisty, M.N.   Bangladesh

c.   Dmitrieva, Rimma   USSR

d.   Alvarez-Lajonchere, Celestino Cuba

e.   Demetriades, Evros   Cyprus (reproduced in
                                     Section VIII)

f.   Abdul Baqi, Nawal   Jordan

g.   Saleh, Noor A.   People's Democratic Republic
                                     of Yemen

h.   Miltenyi, Karoly   Hungary (reproduced in
                                     Section VIII)

i.   Mikhailova, Pavlina   Bulgaria

In this session those seminar participants employed by governments were asked to discuss how research on women and population issues is integrated with policy measures within their own countries. It is interesting to note that many of the authors of the papers are themselves researchers, while at the same time being involved in policy formulation and implementation. This integration at the individual level demonstrates in itself that policy and research can in practice be very closely linked.

Papers

a. Attiya Inayatullah stated that in Pakistan the fact that the Population Division is part of the Ministry for Planning and Development is a clear indication of the decision-maker's recognition that population issues are an important element in development planning. Furthermore, it indicates that in Pakistan, among those in government circles who are concerned with women and population issues, there is an implicit recognition that research is needed and that without reliable research data, the foundation or base of policy efforts will be weak. Further, Inayatullah indicated that research projects on population and women have as an essential component built-in monitoring and flexibility; this permits a continuing review of progress and search for directions that appear to meet the purposes and objectives of expressed policy goals.

Inayatullah then presented some examples of research undertakings and their utilisation.

(i) The Sixth Five Year Plan 1983-88 states in its objectives, for the first time, that the population programme alone is not expected to achieve the demographic objectives of the Plan, and that the Plan's development strategies are equally relevant to these demographic objectives. A methodology is being prepared whereby progress towards policy objectives will be measured through a retrieval system and correlated with expected effects on the fertility situation. The findings will be periodically reviewed and recommendations made in respect of stated policy and actually achieved goals.

(ii) The Population Development Centre of the Population Division has a client record card system which, on a quarterly basis, provides the policy-maker and programme officer with data pertaining to service performance, logistics, supply and distribution, information and education, management functions, community involvement, and financial information. Based on these data, remedial action is identified and taken.

Resources for research being limited, and the usefulness of research being frequently doubted, it is essential that this important output be addressed with the seriousness it warrants. There needs to be a serious dialogue between researchers and policy-makers, and a holistic approach to research which takes into consideration cultural factors.

The Pakistan Government is currently concerned by questions such as:

What are the mechanisms by which the recipient of the programme and the planner can best be involved in research?

How can research be structured at the grass-roots level, with mechanisms for the two-way flow of information?

How long does it normally take for research reports to be published?

How can research findings be made easier to comprehend and more convincing?

Is there money available for innovative research undertaken on a pilot basis?

b. M.N. Chisty of Bangladesh described how research and evaluation studies on women's issues and related demographic issues have been conducted through several institutes and organisations.

The National Institute of Population Research and Training (NIPORT), under the Ministry of Health and Population Control, was set up to conduct research and training on population matters. NIPORT is responsible for overall co-ordination of research activities on population-related matters. A Management Information System (MIS) was also established, under the same ministry, for direct evaluation and monitoring of field activities.

Other institutes specifically devoted to research are the Population Study Centres in the Bangladesh Institute of Development Study (BIDS), the International Centre for Diarrhoea/Diseases Research, and the Bangladesh Fertility Research Programme which is responsible for undertaking research on the efficiency of different contraceptive methods. The Population Planning Section and External Evaluation Unit of the Planning Commission have also undertaken evaluation studies on various women's programmes. In addition, Women For Women, Concerned Women, UNICEF (Bangladesh) and several other agencies and organisations have been conducting studies on women's roles, as related to demographic, social and economic issues.

c. Rimma Dmietrieva gave some examples to show how in the USSR, policies and research on women and population are closely linked. In 1976, the government invited various institutes to conduct research into current fertility trends and suggest appropriate population policies measures.

One important finding was that women did not expect to have as many children as they wanted. One focus of population measures has therefore been to assist married women to achieve their desired family size. Since 1981 measures aimed at providing better conditions for population reproduction have been introduced gradually, and it is noticeable that increases in the birth rate have been most significant in areas where such measures have been implemented. Next year a survey is planned to find out which population groups have been most affected by these measures, and to identify other measures which might have some impact. Research is also planned to find out which social groups tend to take extended maternity leave.

Dmietrieva concluded that population policy can be effective particularly if monitored by research and up-dated and refined periodically.

d. Celestino Alvarez-Lajonchere pointed out that the rapid decline in fertility in Cuba was not related to any government policy of fertility reduction. The principal concern of government was not to control demographic processes but to produce basic structural changes which would lead to development. This was done by means of such measures as the development of a free National Health Service, literacy campaigns, and programmes to increase the level of women's education and training. It is well known, however, that such measures have an important influence on demographic behaviour. The government can only accept this result and be ready to respond to the situation if necessary, since changes in demographic behaviour will undoubtedly continue.

Just after the Revolution - 25 years ago - there was little useful research to help policy-makers. In recent years in Cuba, two censuses and some important surveys have provided the government with enough data to guide the political decision-making process and evaluate the process of change. Some demographic findings arising from these surveys were presented in this seminar.

The specialised demographic centre, CEDEM, university teams, and the Department of State Statistics Committee collaborate with one another. There is a central office in the Academy of Science to co-ordinate the most important research and to look for ways of applying the results rapidly. The scarce resources available are being applied in well inter-related studies. However, there are still no in-depth studies in Cuba on divorce and adolescent pregnancy, and these are much needed.

Alvarez-Lajonchere suggested that for developing countries the first solid step to take in data collection is to produce vital statistics, since these can be used as powerful tools for simple but useful research. The collection, processing and, of course, use of basic statistical data for the whole country is the key starting point.

e. Evros Demetriades stated that the Government of Cyprus had recognised the value and usefulness of research in the formulation, implementation, and follow-up of its economic and social development efforts and the assessment of future perspectives. The complex inter-relationships and linkages that exist between the socio-economic and demographic aspects of development in a country need to be studied in depth in order to achieve the maximum results from available resources.

Some of the major research undertaken in Cyprus in the past decade has centred on population, the employment status of women, and the socio-economic factors related to female labour force participation (see Section III.3). While it is difficult to document the direct utilisation of the research findings, perhaps their most important contribution has been to create an increased awareness of the importance of integrating human resources factors into development planning. Indirect utilisation of the results can be seen in the policies incorporated into the Development Plan to improve the position of women in the labour market, to upgrade child-care facilities, to help solve the growing problem of the educated unemployed, and to rectify potential imbalances between the demand and supply of various skills in the labour market. Research in these fields has also contributed to the improvement of the statistical base, and to the refinement of the data and methodologies employed. This includes among other things a newly-designed sample survey which laid the foundations for a reliable and cost-effective monthly time-series on employment which can better serve exercises in human resources planning.

A multi-round demographic survey has been conducted to provide data on levels, trends and determinants of fertility, mortality and internal migration and to shed light on the interaction between demographic characteristics and socio-economic variables such as employment, social class and educational level. The survey provided excellent data on the above topics, which have been utilised extensively by various government departments in the formulation of measures and policies related to population and welfare issues.

f. In her paper, Nawal Abdul Baqi pointed out that recent wars with Israel have caused substantial variations in the population and land area of Jordan; this situation must therefore be kept in mind when discussing women's and population issues in Jordan.

Despite these difficult conditions, the government succeeded in carrying out a household population census in 1979 and a number of socio-economic surveys, including a demographic survey, in 1981. Indeed Jordanian law stipulates that at least once every 10 years separate censuses should be carried out for industry, agriculture and population and housing.

The natural growth rate of the population in Jordan is currently one of the highest in the world (3.8 per cent); in 1979, 53.2 per cent of the population was under 15 years of age. Recent expansion of the economy combined with an outflow of Jordanian workers to other countries has resulted in shortages of certain types of skilled labour. This has led to the importation of foreign workers; in 1980, about 15 per cent of the East Bank labour force was foreign.

In 1977, a Department of Women's Affairs was established in the Ministry of Labour to deal with problems relating to Jordanian women and to encourage greater participation by women in the process of socio-economic development. Although female participation rates have increased slightly in recent years, according to official statistics only about 14 per cent of women of working age were in the East Bank labour force in 1980. The Ministry of Labour is currently working on a survey of training and employment opportunities for women in Jordan. The Ministry is seeking to provide incentives and facilities to encourage more women to participate in the labour force; this includes encouraging productive activities which can be done at home.

g. The paper by Noor Saleh of the People's Democratic Republic of Yemen emphasised the importance of research for the implementation of government policies concerning women. The 1970 Constitution laid the basis of government policy on women. It gave all citizens legal equality which implied a formal change in women's legal status from the previous interpretation of Koranic law or Shariat. All citizens were granted the right to work, and women were called upon to enter social production. Among the measures taken to encourage this were the expansion of the women's union to assist women in gaining their rights, the extension of education and literacy programmes to women, the granting of paid maternity leave, and the provision of child-care facilities for women workers.

The Family Law of 1974 attempted to bring judicial practice in line with the principles of the state by removing traditional familial controls over women and establishing full equality of rights between the sexes in marriage. The Law made arranged and child marriages illegal, fixed the minimum age for marriage at 16 for girls and 18 for boys, and removed men's right to polygamy and divorce by repudiation.

The female labour force participation rate in 1980 was estimated at about 20 per cent. Although high for a Muslim country, this still means that a great many women are not officially active. The reasons go back to the belief that a woman's place is at home, and bringing up children. Wives may opt to stay at home rather than go to work to protect their marriage, since opting for work may weaken the relationship between the wife and her husband. Studies need to be conducted to investigate how government can best encourage and facilitate the participation of women in productive activities, and how participation is being influenced by traditional ties, marriage, illiteracy, education, and family planning. Research should be carried out to examine possible improvements in female working conditions to enable them to overcome the prevailing difficulties. The government would then be in a better position to adopt additional measures to promote the overall goal of equality between men and women in work and in the family.

h. The paper by Karoly Miltenyi outlined the organisational scheme in Hungary which ensures a permanent communication and dialogue between policy-makers/planners and professional research workers.

The central organ for long-term planning and policy formulation is the National Planning Office. Policy formulation involves committees, consisting of the representatives and experts of relevant state organs, and of social and scientific organisations. Population policy formulation takes place within the framework of the Committee for General Long-term Planning, which also deals with other major topics such as health, education, housing, and employment.

The subcommittee for population makes extensive use of the results of demographic research. This is facilitated by the fact that the priorities of the scientific research, are determined or at least strongly influenced by the requirements of government and policy-formulating organs. Population projections constitute the basis of medium- and long-term planning in many fields; for the purposes of housing and consumption policy, projections on households/families are used.

Survey results have also been found to be useful in policy formulation in Hungary. For example, longitudinal surveys indicate that the housing conditions of young couples have a significant impact both on the number of children they plan and on the actual number they have. The most important factor is whether the couple has a separate dwelling either at marriage or shortly after marriage, i.e. in the potentially most fertile period. For this reason, housing policy measures give preference to young newly-wed couples.

h. Pavlina Mihkailova explained that in Bulgaria research and policy are closely linked. She herself is part of a research group at the Bulgarian Academy of Sciences, which advises the government on problems of reproduction and public health.

The general framework is that basic research is conducted by the Bulgarian Academy of Science and more applied research is done at industrial research centres. Together these two types of research service as a basis for long-term planning. Research on problems of social policy is inter-disciplinary, combining both economic and social approaches.

Research results are taken into account by the government when making decisions, so there is a direct link between research and government policies.

Discussion

In the discussion that followed, it was pointed out that there are great differences between countries as far as the availability of basic data is concerned. In some countries, no census has been taken for decades. Such a situation handicaps the planning process enormously, and means that research may have a rather different orientation from that in countries where regular, reliable census and survey statistics are available.

It was also pointed out that in countries where most of the research on women and population is being done either within government departments or at the request of government, research is likely to be responding to a felt need within the government and its chances of being utilised are good.

Participants from large countries with considerable regional differences emphasised the importance of research and planning being done at the regional level. Information systems should feed back to local organisations so that problems can be solved on the spot. Long distances and problems of communication and transport were also cited as difficulties for researchers in such countries.

The view was expressed that there should be more systematic study of specific interventions, and also that such studies could compare how reactions to a similar intervention may differ between regions.

VII. CONCLUSIONS

The following conclusions were prepared by a drafting committee (see section 1.8) and agreed to by seminar participants.

<u>Preamble</u>

1. During the last decade, considerable attention has been directed towards questions related to the roles and status of women - especially since the United Nations International World Conference of the International Women's Year (Mexico City, 1975) and the World Conference of the UN Decade for Women (Copenhagen, 1980). Partly as a result, it is now widely recognised that social, political and economic policies and changes may have adverse effects on men and women, and that a conscious effort should be made to improve the relative position of women in families, in the economy, and in society. It is also widely believed that labour force activity patterns of women are interrelated with family size, family health, family structure, and other demographic factors such as migration - in brief, that there is a critical interplay between the productive and reproductive roles of women.

2. This interplay between the roles of women in regard to participation in economic and social life of the community and the nation and their responsibilities towards the family as mothers varies in different socio-economic systems, at different stages of socio-economic development, and in different cultural contexts.

a. In the developing world, over 80 per cent of the population live in countries which put reduction of fertility and the promotion and practice of planned smaller families at the top of the agenda of national priorities; it is considered that rapid labour force growth complicates efforts in terms of policy and action programmes to ensure women a fair deal in the fields of, inter alia, education, training, employment and career development - and thus in the fulfilment of aspirations relating to their own self-development. While socio-economic development may be expected to lead to a reduction in fertility - as experience in industrialised countries has shown and as is indeed recommended in the World Population Plan of Action adopted by the World Population Conference (Bucharest, 1974) - a number of countries have embarked on national programmes of birth or family planning as an integral part of national development policies.

b. Industrialised countries, on the other hand, experience low fertility, in many cases below replacement level. They are seeking, on the whole, to follow policies which facilitate the reconciliation of family formation and participation of women in socio-economic life. Among the industrialised countries, the focus in this seminar was on socialist countries. In these countries, it was noted, there are high rates of women's economic participation. Their governments provide assistance to the family and working woman, to enable her to combine motherhood with labour activity.

3. These above concerns have also been stressed in the preparatory work for the Third World Conference on Women (Nairobi, 1985) as well as for the International Population Conference (Mexico, 1984).

Methodological issues

4. Participation of women in the labour force seems to be increasing significantly with social and economic development. It is widely recognised however (for example in the 1980 Copenhagen Conference), that currently available statistics on female labour force participation are often affected by sex stereo-typing and that many countries under-report women's economic contribution, especially as far as unpaid family labour is concerned. A general revision of the conceptual framework of labour force activity is needed. Needless to say, some parallel improvements are called for in the measurement of men's and especially children's employment. Several labour force measures may be defined so as to meet diverse planning needs, distinguishing, for example, between waged work and other work (paid or unpaid) which contributes to GNP, as in the currently accepted international definition, as well as some relevant house-hold services which are often commercialised and so included in GNP in industrial economies. Definitions and survey question-naires distinguishing between different kinds of work activity should increase accuracy of measurement and facilitate comparability between surveys. Research and experimentation to improve labour force surveys and data collection techniques deserve the most careful attention, especially in the ILO. The continuing inadequacy of data on women's work in many countries limits policy formulation and research on the relationship between women's labour force participation and fertility.

5. Numerous conferences (including the Copenhagen and Mexico World Conferences on the UN Decade for Women) have repeatedly recommended that evaluation should be made of the implicit economic contributions to the economy and family welfare of unpaid, non-market activities. The possible importance of such evaluations for women's status, measurement of national income, legal claims, etc., was also recognised in the present seminar. However, because of the major methodological, conceptual and measurement difficulties involved in making such evaluations, it was felt that research was required to help develop appropriate methodologies and to assess the usefulness and shortcomings of such evaluations.

6.   Applied research must be grounded in basic research. Basic research is important, for example investigations into the circumstances under which various social changes result in one kind of reproductive behaviour or another.   Appropriate theoretical frameworks need to be developed to guide the design and interpretation of research, whether basic or applied.

7.   The usefulness of holistic/interdisciplinary/integrated approaches should be emphasised.   Research programmes can be formulated and their results analysed only in the context of a given socio-economic system.   Historical and cultural factors have to be considered too.   Thus, research on women's status and activities should put women's roles and activities into the context of family, community, local employment conditions, culture, and socio-economic system.

8.   The need for case and in-depth studies was stressed by the participants.   However, if possible the results of such studies should be evaluated and analysed in combination with statistics of a comprehensive and/or representative nature.   If this kind of linkage is not possible, special caution is needed to avoid unwarranted generalisations not supported by adequate empirical evidence.   At the same time, in-depth case studies may be used to gain additional insights into problematic and complex issues and also to test the validity of survey data and other statistics, such as, for example, KAP (knowledge, attitude and practice of family planning) surveys.

9.   In household surveys, all members of the household who are the subject of the research should be interviewed personally, if possible. When a key respondent is selected, income, family composition and knowledge of the subject under study should be considered rather than specifying that the key respondent must be a man.   In any case it should be emphasised that designating a key respondent or head of household does not imply any value judgement. It is a technical requirement of household surveys.

10.   Time use studies should be conducted on a small scale from time to time to supplement information from large surveys, to help in the design of large-scale employment surveys, which cannot be too detailed, and as part of detailed research enquiries.   However, it must be recognised that time use studies are costly and time-consuming and involve a number of methodological problems such as simultaneous activities and respondents' lack of awareness of exact time allocations.   Further research is needed to assess the accuracy of such time use surveys, to solve methodological problems, and, above all, to clarify and increase the analytical usefulness of these surveys.

11.   Survey instruments, manuals, and other research tools usually need to be adapted to country-specific conditions. Local researchers should be encouraged to undertake this task.

12.   There is an urgent need to develop appropriate tools for assisting in setting up, monitoring and evaluating action intervention projects.   International comparative research, such as in the ILO research programme, is useful in providing methodological developments and should be encouraged.

Utilisation of research

13.   Before embarking on the collection of new data, further analysis of existing data is normally useful and will often be all that is needed.   Data from censuses and surveys are often not adequately analysed, analysis frequently going no further than the provision of summary tables.   In this context, effective storage and access to data (through use of appropriate technology, training and institutional development) is of the utmost importance.

14.   A comprehensive stock-taking of relevant research already undertaken needs to be carried out as the basis for drawing up an agenda for additional research of policy relevance. Experience shows that too often studies are undertaken without taking into account previous research.

15.   In order to increase the effectiveness and utilisation of research for policy purposes, close co-operation and collaboration between researchers and policy-makers/planners/administrators is essential when formulating research objectives and design. Utilisation is also furthered by frequent discussion of progress on a research project so as to maintain continuous interest among policy-makers and planners.   Close collaboration with other groups involved in the subject of the research, such as women's organisations, community groups, trade unions, and employers, is also important for its eventual utilisation.   However, the primary responsibility for the design and conduct of research should rest with researchers.

16.   There should be a concern on the part of researchers, when suggesting policy and programme interventions, about their feasibility and social relevance.

17.   To increase the effectiveness of research studies and to reduce possible duplication, findings should be disseminated to a wide spectrum of users including relevant government agencies, subjects of the research, trade unions, employers' organisations, women's organisations, community and local organisations, research institutions, etc.   In this context, research results should be presented as simply and briefly as possible in order to increase the chances of their being utilised.

Knowledge gaps and research needs

18.   Discrimination against women is still widespread in practice in many countries.   This is particularly true in employment, remuneration, education and training, health care and the like, as well as within the family.   As far as economic activity is concerned, the reasons for this discrimination are complex and include the labour market structure in conjunction with cultural factors.   Research is required to understand the underlying causes, which may vary from country to country.   This research should be so designed as to contribute to the identification and design of policies and action programmes aimed at eliminating sex inequalities.   Research is also needed on the effects of relevant legislation, including the ILO conventions and standards.

19.   Family responsibilities are an important limitation on women's ability to participate in economic activity.   They also limit the type of employment which women undertake and the skills they acquire.   The unequal sharing between men and women of household tasks and child-care is a general problem. Studies need to be undertaken on practical measures for reducing the constraints of family responsibilities which prevent the full and equal participation of women in economic and social life in the context of the limited financial resources of developing countries.   In this context, it might be useful to draw upon the experience of the socialist countries.

20.   Development of appropriate methodologies is needed both for assessing the demographic impact of socio-economic policies and programmes and for drawing up criteria and guidelines for harmonising, as much as possible, these policies with the goals of population policies.   Conversely, the social and economic consequences of current and prospective demographic trends should be taken into account for integrated population and development policies and planning at national and sub-national levels.

21.   The multiple roles of women as workers inside and outside the home, as wives, mothers, kin and community members are at the centre of both population and labour issues.   In addition, it is necessary to consider corresponding male roles and the relationships between women and men.   In particular, the factors encouraging and facilitating sexual equality and the sharing of resources and responsibilities, both inside and outside the home, need to be examined.   Sexual equality in leisure time can be seen as part of the concern for equality in working life, and is an aspect which studies should not overlook.

22.   Family planning programmes and population policies are often unsuccessful due to a lack of understanding and knowledge of the social, economic and cultural factors determining fertility behaviour.   Studies and programmes need to be country- and

culture-specific. Changes in fertility and family planning acceptance rates should be analysed and viewed within this broader framework.

23. It is important to understand the mechanisms of fertility decision-making and the factors influencing it, possibly through in-depth case studies. In this respect, it is important to mention that the experience with KAP (knowledge, attitude and practice) surveys shows that results from such surveys can be misleading because of the gap between knowledge, stated intentions and actual practice.

24. In population and development action programmes (for example, schemes for women's employment and income generation, or family planning and health service delivery at the local level), research should be a built-in component, where feasible, in their design, implementation, monitoring, and evaluation.

25. The importance of community influence on population growth, women's participation in the labour force, etc., has been noted. Studies should be undertaken to help understand the mechanism through which the community influences such issues as labour supply and population growth. Such studies will be particularly useful if they are integrated with development activities at the community level, such as income generation schemes for women, co-operative schemes, health and family planning programmes, etc.

26. In many countries, the expression "family planning" is misunderstood as a means to reduce fertility and family size only; hence research is needed to design better the messages and broaden the approaches of family planning programmes to include communication and education in family life relations between husband and wife and between parents and children.

27. In many countries teenage fertility is important. Given its strong adverse effects on lifetime fertility, health, education, training, and future economic participation, it needs to be researched. The introduction of sex education (taken in the broad sense) in schools, vocational training institutes and work settings is one important measure in this context, and should include a research component.

28. Research effort is needed to examine the terms and conditions of work in labour-intensive export-oriented industries in developing countries where women workers often predominate.

29. The performance of development programmes and projects tends to be uneven. The factors underlying the successes and failures need to be analysed to provide lessons for planners and administrators.

30. Female heads of households are an important disadvantaged group in a number of countries. Their position is particularly precarious because they frequently have limited employment opportunities and are often the sole supporters of their children. Many diverse circumstances are responsible for women being the head of the houshold, and research is required to understand this phenomenon more fully and to help in devising appropriate policies and programmes.

31. Migrant women workers constitute a particularly vulnerable group as they are often in occupations which are not effectively protected by labour laws (such as domestic work) and they may also lack family support. Policy-oriented studies are needed on how to ameliorate the situation of these women.

32. In many countries, women and children are left behind by male migrants (internal and external). The effects of this phenomenon are not adequately understood and need to be researched.

Conclusions for the ILO and UN organisations

33. The ILO should intensify its activities for the reduction of discrimination and the promotion of equal opportunity for women in employment. This may include:

a. reviewing and studying the effective application of relevant international labour standards designed to improve women's working conditions;

b. undertaking research and action programmes to expand, diversify and improve income-generating and training opportunities for women;

c. studying in depth national policies and programmes to reduce discrimination and inequality based on sex, including women migrant workers and women with family responsibilities;

d. undertaking studies of the sexual division of labour in both private and public sectors and of its effect on the implementation of equal pay for work of equal value;

e. studying measures designed to reconcile the worker and mother roles of women such as maternity protection, child-care facilities, flexible hours, part-time work, paternity leave, etc.;

f. studying (i) women's participation in trade unions at different levels of decision-making; (ii) the role of trade unions in dealing with discriminatory practices against women workers.

34. The roles of the woman as worker and as mother/housewife are closely linked and are at the centre of both popu-

lation and labour issues. Accordingly, the ILO should continue to be concerned with the ways in which women's motherhood and fertility interact with their position in the workforce. Similarly, the UN and international donor agencies providing assistance in the area of fertility and family planning (such as UNFPA) should be concerned with the vital links between women's work (both inside and outside the home) and fertility behaviour.

35.   The ILO should continue its action-oriented research and development of methodologies in various fields of population and development as identified above, in particular:

a.   improved definition, measurement and analysis of women's and children's labour force participation and their contribution to the national economy;

b.   development of practical methodologies to integrate more effectively population factors into development policies, planning and programmes at national and sub-national levels;

c.   designing and testing research approaches to community and local-level development and interventions/changes (such as women's income generation schemes, co-operatives, rural electrification) which may make a critical contribution towards improving family welfare and reducing fertility;

d.   continued production of guidelines for research and materials of practical use to researchers;

e.   continued study of the relationship between women's work roles and fertility.

36.   In recent years, a rather narrow approach to population issues has been adopted by donor agencies providing international population assistance. A more comprehensive approach is needed, along the lines recommended by the World Population Plan of Action, particularly for countries committed to reducing fertility levels as national policy.

37.   There is a need for better co-operation and co-ordination among various UN and other international agencies in the field of women's employment and population issues.

VIII. SELECTED PAPERS

1.   Female Labour Force Participation: ILO Research on
      Conceptual and Measurement Issues - Richard Anker
      Paper reported in Section III.1

Introduction

    With the overall objective of improving our understanding of
the complex interrelationships between female employment and
demographic variables such as fertility, family planning and
health, the ILO/UNFPA research programme on "Women's Roles
and Demographic Change" has concentrated much of its attention
on the development of appropriate research methodologies.   In
particular, a multidisciplinary approach was adopted which
included   integrated   quantitative-qualitative   studies;   both
individual and household survey questionnaires favoured by
economists and statisticians as well as the in-depth qualitative
case study approach favoured by anthropologists were used.
Thus, "model" questionnaires (Anker, 1980), a quantative-
qualitative study design (Anker, 1982), a case study framework
(Oppong, 1980) and case study field guides (Oppong and
Church, 1981;   Nag, Anker and Khan, 1982) were developed.
In the current paper, one (major) methodological aspect of the
ILO's research programme will be described: Improving the
measurement of female labour force participation.

The problem

    It is widely recognised that currently available statistics
from the developing world on female labour force participation
are inaccurate, grossly underreporting female labour force
activity in many of these countries.   As reviewed in a recent
paper (Anker, 1983a), there are believed to be several reasons
for this underreporting of female labour force participation.
    First, the internationally accepted definition of labour force
participation and its interpretation is often thought to be the
cause.   According to the ILO, labour force activity is defined
as follows:
    All persons of either sex who furnish the supply of
    labour for the production of economic goods and
    services as defined by the United Nations system of
    national accounts and balances. (Recommendations of
    the Thirteenth Conference of Labour Statisticians,
    1982).

    According to these systems [of national income
    accounts], the production of economic goods and
    services should include all production and processing
    of primary products whether for the market, for
    barter or for own consumption. (ILO, 1982)

Obviously, market-oriented activities related to wage or salary employment and/or enterprises are labour force activities; so should be activities oriented to self-consumption such as subsistence agriculture, home construction and improvement, milking animals and processing food for family use. Yet, national practices vary so greatly both with respect to national income statistics and labour force definitions as to cause great variability in the measurement of the female labour force both across countries and across time within particular countries.

A few examples illustrate this situation fairly well. A survey of national practices in 70 developing countries on the inclusion in national income of the value from subsistence activities revealed that 71 per cent of the countries included the imputed value of forestry products (e.g. cutting wood), 39 per cent food processing, 50 per cent handicrafts and 7 per cent water carrying (Blades, 1975). In Fiji, persons have to tend more than ten chickens for this activity to be considered as a labour force activity. In India, the female labour activity rate as recorded on national censuses went from about 28 per cent in 1961 to about 12 per cent in 1971 to about 14 per cent in 1981; the 32nd round of the National Sample Survey created a new non-labour force activity entitled "attended domestic duties and was also engaged in free collection of goods, sewing, weaving, etc. for household use" (Sarvekshana, 1980).

One possible explanation for anomalies such as these is that there is a straightforward sex bias in both the international definition and in its interpretation at the national level. While the severe restriction on length in this paper precludes a lengthy discussion on this issue, suffice it to say that there is a systematic exclusion from (inclusion in) the labour force and national income of activities typically performed by women (men) almost as if labour force/non-labour force distinctions were drawn up with prior information on the sexual division of labour - and despite the fact that in large parts of the developing world the distinction between economic/labour force activities and non-economic/ non-labour force activities is somewhat arbitrary. The fact is that in most of the Third World - especially among the poor - virtually all adults (as well as their children) make significant contributions to meeting the family's basic needs.

A second factor believed to be important in causing female labour force data to be unrealistically low is that women tend to be only marginally involved in the data collection, as survey designers, interviewers and respondents. As a result, the preconceived notion of women as "housewives" which men may be more likely to hold than women, is believed to affect how survey questionnaires are designed, how survey questions are actually asked by interviewers, as well as how respondents reply to these questions. Although there is little statistical evidence to indicate the degree to which male interviewers, male respondents and male survey designers bias labour force statistics, it would seem (as discussed above) that both the internationally accepted definition of labour force participation and its application in national censuses and labour force surveys are made worse by the relatively small input of women in the data collection process.

A third factor believed to be important is that labour force questions and questionnaires tend to be inappropriately worded and constructed for obtaining accurate information for women, frequently beginning with a fairly simple question (which usually can be reduced to one key word or phrase such as "work", "job", "main activity", "secondary activity", "economic activity", "pay or profit") in order to divide the population into two groups: (1) economically active and (2) "economically" inactive. (Note that unemployment is ignored in this discussion.) The simplicity of these questions is crucial in my opinion in producing the relatively poor labour force data for women that are collected. It is not reasonable to expect respondents to provide accurate information about what is essentially an ambiguous concept (especially for subsistence type activities) when the questions they are being asked are so simple. Under these circumstances, it is hardly surprising that stereotypes such as the "non-working" "housewife" frequently predominate.

ILO research activities

Given the situation as outlined above, a desire to understand demographic interrelationships with female activity, along with a desire to improve the quality of national data on the female labour force, it was decided to undertake several related methodological research activities on measurement of female labour force activity as part of the ILO's research programme.

a. Major country studies using detailed activity/ time use approach

The major multidisciplinary studies undertaken in India, Egypt and Bangladesh (some preliminary results are described in the seminar proceedings in the next paper by Khan and Dastidar) have used an activity/time use approach. Instead of asking respondents whether household members had "worked" or had a "job" or using other such key words, each of these studies collected detailed data on the activities engaged in by household members. In this way, no a priori assumptions were made as to what is and is not a labour force activity; rather respondents simply had to report what they did, they did not have to reply to nebulous key words or concepts. In this way, it becomes relatively easy to: define labour force participation in different ways for different purposes after the survey is completed and the data is processed, and to obtain additional information about particular activities (such as whether they involved receipt of wage payments on cash income from sales, amount of time spent on activity, whether income/wages received directly for activity, presence and interference of children, proximity to the house, etc.) Availability of such information could change, for example, our perception of socio-economic-demographic relationships as it is quite possible that certain types of activities, differentiated by one or more of the characteristics noted above, are related to fertility or infant mortality whereas a crude dichotomous measure of labour force participation as currently defined (whether or nor accurately measured) may not.

These detailed enquiries of what women and other household members are doing are using several types of data collection techniques. Anthropologists who are living for approximately one year in several villages in each sample country, are collecting activity/time use data through observation, as well as through recall each fortnight or month. These data should provide highly accurate accounts of female activity patterns. In addition, in a larger sample of approximately 1,000 households in each sample country, multi-round (two or three round) surveys are being conducted; these surveys include activity/ time use schedules where respondents are asked to recall which of approximately 30 activities household members performed over the past season.

b. Improving accuracy of female labour force data collected on national surveys and censuses

As a follow-up to the Egyptian and Indian studies which use a detailed activity/time use approach, we have been attempting to increase knowledge on how to improve the collection of data on the female labour force in national censuses and labour force surveys where detailed activity/time use surveys are not appropriate, in our opinion, as they are too costly (requiring a great deal of interviewing time) and too difficult to conduct (requiring highly trained and dedicated interviewers and supervisors). Such in-depth studies, however, remain useful tools for research studies and as quality checks for larger surveys (see Jain (1983) for discussion of such a quality check being carried out for the National Sample Survey in India).

To provide statistically valid insights into the effect some factors have on the data obtained concerning the female labour force, the ILO research programme is conducting methodological tests in Egypt (in collaboration with CAPMAS, Central Agency for Public Mobilisation and Statistics) and in India (in collaboration with ORG, Operations Research Group). These methods tests will use equal numbers of male and female interviewers; equal numbers of male and female respondents as well as self and proxy respondents will be interviewed; and equal numbers of different types of short questionnaires (key word type question- naire, activity type questionnaire, combined key word-activity type questionnaire) of 10-15 minutes duration will be administered. Since replicate (i.e. statistically identical) samples to those of the detailed in-depth studies described in the previous subsection will be used, it will be possible to observe:

(i)   What type of short questionnaire provides the more

accurate data on female labour force activity? In particular, do short activity-type schedules or key word questionnaires provide more accurate data; how do these labour force data differ as compared to that collected by anthropologists and survey interviewers on the major country studies described in the last subsection?

(ii) Does the sex of the interviewer affect the reported female labour force activity rate?

(iii) Do proxy-respondents (i.e. persons who answer for someone else) provide different responses on female labour force activity as compared to self-respondents (i.e. persons who answer for themselves)? Do male and female proxy-respondents provide different responses?

For a detailed description of the labour force methods test being conducted in Egypt and India, readers are referred to Anker (1983b).

c. Defining labour force participation and evaluating the economic value of "non-labour force" activities

The critical review of current data collection techniques reported in Anker (1983a), parts of which are summarised above, concluded that confusion with the current internationally accepted definition of labour force participation is to a significant extent due to: (1) its reliance on a simple (in or out) dichotomy between labour force participation and non-labour force participation and (2) an inherent ambiguity in having consistent and logical distinctions between labour force and non-labour force activities when subsistence type activities are concerned. With these difficulties in mind, it was recommended that government statistical offices should collect sufficient data in order to be in a position to report several labour force measures - partly because there cannot be one correct definition of the labour force, partly because there are diverse planning needs which are best served by several labour force measures, partly in order to reflect more accurately women's true economic contributions, partly in order to increase comparability of labour force data over time within and between nations, and partly to reflect more fully the degree to which basic needs are being met. Specifically, four labour force definitions at increasing levels of inclusivity were suggested - "paid labour force" (basically wage and salary employees), "market-oriented labour force" (employees plus persons engaged in activities where products are sold), "ILO labour force" (current definition), "extended labour force" (which would include persons performing activities not counted in national income but which nonetheless make a significant contribution to meeting the family's basic needs and which are generally purchased in developed countries). We also suggested that reported labour force data should be subdivided according to whether persons are full- or part-time participants.

In light of the inherent ambiguity for subsistence activities in defining labour force participation, the fact that these activities are done mainly by women and are often unpaid, and the fact that they are crucial to meeting the basic needs of the family, the ILO research programme has to a very limited extent been engaged in studying issues related to evaluating the economic value of unpaid household and subsistence activities. The policy significance and usefulness of such evaluations are quite important. They are likely to affect: divorce settlements, accident settlements, future developments in national income account statistics and labour force statistics, government perspectives on the meeting of basic needs and overall welfare levels, as well as general perceptions of the relative contributions toward "total output" made by different segments of population such as women and children.

Luisella Goldschmidt-Clermont (1982) has reviewed previous evaluations in developed countries of unpaid household activities along with the methodologies used to make these evaluations. Although there is great variation in results due to variation in the methodologies and assumptions used, in general unpaid activities tended to add up to around 25-50 per cent of the measured GNP. Presently, in collaboration with Goldschmidt-Clermont, this review is being extended to developing countries. Not too surprisingly, only a few such evaluations seem to have been done in developing countries. A new evaluation is now being done as part of our major joint study in India with ORG in order to observe the appropriateness of these methodologies and their assumptions for the developing world, and to determine if guidelines for such evaluations can be developed.

Bibliography

Anker, R. 1980. *Research on women's roles and demographic change: Survey questionnaires for households, women, men and communities with background explanations*. Geneva, ILO.

---. 1982. "Demographic change and the role of women: A research programme in developing countries", in R. Anker, M. Buvinic and N. Youssef (eds.): *Women's roles and population trends in the Third World*. London, Croom Helm.

---. 1983a. *Female labour force activity in developing countries: A critique of current data collection techniques*. Geneva, ILO; mimeographed World Employment Programme research working paper.

---. 1983b. *Effect on reported levels of female labour force participation in developing countries of questionnaire design, sex of interviewer and sex/proxy status of respondent: Description of a methodological field experiment*. Geneva, ILO; mimeographed World Employment Programme research working paper.

Blades, D. 1975. *Non-monetary (subsistence) activities in the national accounts of developing countries*. Paris, OECD.

Goldschmidt-Clermont, L. 1982. *Unpaid work in the household*. Geneva, ILO.

Jain, D. 1983. "Co-opting women's work into the statistical system - some Indian milestones", in *Samyashakti: A Journal of Women's Studies*, Vol. 1, No. 1, July.

Nag, M., Anker, R. and Khan, M.E. 1982. *A guide to anthropological study of women's roles and demographic change in India*. Geneva, ILO; mimeographed World Employment Programme research working paper.

Oppong, C. 1980. *A synopsis of seven roles and status of women: An outline of a conceptual and methodological approach*. Geneva, ILO; mimeographed World Employment Programme research working paper.

Oppong, C. and Church, K. 1981. *A field guide to research on seven roles of women: Focused biographies*. Geneva, ILO; mimeographed World Employment Programme research working paper.

ILO. 1982. *Amended draft resolution concerning statistics of the economically active population, employment, unemployment and underemployment*, Thirteeenth International Conference of Labour Statisticians; mimeograph.

Sarvekshana. 1980. *Journal of the National Sample Survey Organisation*, Vol. III. No. 3.

2.　Methodological Insights from Collaborative Indian studies
　　- M.E. Khan and S.K. Ghosh Dastidar
　　Paper reported in Section III.1.

Introduction

The present paper provides some insights into the merits and problems of an experimental study carried out by Operations Research Group which attempts to integrate two hitherto diagonally opposite approaches - the sample survey and case study approaches. Sample surveys use probability models to select a sizeable sample in such a way that the selected sample represents the population as a whole and thus the findings of the study could be applied to the entire universe with a certain degree of confidence. The economists, demographers, and statisticians are the champions of this approach, and have successfully contributed in generating useful data at the macro level. In the case study approach, on the other hand, only a limited number of sample units are selected on a more or less purposive basis and such studies are mostly confined to one or two villages or communities. Sociologists and anthropologists are the proponents of this approach and are responsible for contributing some of the finest pieces of work explaining the social behaviour at the macro level. However, both these approaches have inherent limitations. While the sample survey approach is criticised for being too generalistic without explaining the processes of social change and human behaviour in a dynamic situation, the case study approach is rejected by survey experts and to a great extent by the policy makers also, on the grounds that the findings are based on very small and purposively selected samples, and hence the findings cannot be generalised. The prejudices against each other among the followers of these two approaches have prevented them from working together to understand and explain the social processes at the community level.

Given this scenario, the ILO study on "Women's Roles and Demographic Change" is unique in many respects. (For the details of this study and suggested approach, see Richard Anker, 1982). It integrates the two approaches to generate complementary information on family decision-making processes. It will be interesting to see how far the three studies in India, Bangladesh and Egypt succeed and to what extent they can come out with a better methodology to answer some of the unanswered issues regarding demographic behaviour. The challenge is more in terms of developing and testing a new methodology which could be used in different socio-economic and cultural settings rather than only answering a few questions.

The Indian Study

The Indian part of the study, undertaken by Operations

Research Group (ORG), Baroda was conducted in Uttar Pradesh - the largest state of the country with a population of 111 million. The anthropological part of the study in this state was conducted in three villages - two of which were located in western and one in the eastern part of Uttar Pradesh. In addition, one urban centre, i.e. Lucknow, the capital of the state, was also included. In each of the selected villages, one trained female anthropologist was posted to collect the relevant information from 25 families selected from different class and caste groups. From each of these families, two sets of data were gathered - one by repeat visits on every fifteenth day to record the "yesterday" time use data along with information on sickness in the family and expenditure on education, health, clothes, etc. The other set of data was obtained by detailed discussions and participant observation with the main informant and other family members on the following issues:

a. Nutrition and food habits of females and males;
b. Education of females and males;
c. Reproductive history and health care of females and males;
d. Activities/work of females and males;
e. Control over income and assets by females and males;
f. Aspects of child-bearing and birth planning: attitudes, practices and decision making;
g. Aspects of marriage and divorce: attitudes, practices and decision making;
h. Conditions of elderly, widowed and divorced/separated females and males, and
i. Number of daughters/sons and socio-economic status of household.

To facilitate the data collection and to ensure that a minimum amount of information is collected from all the selected households, a guideline for in-depth interviews was prepared and given to all the investigators (Nag, Anker and Khan, 1982).

To allow the generalisation of the findings of these case studies, a large-scale sample survey has been conducted in villages surrounding those selected for in-depth study (for the detailed survey questionnaire, see Anker, 1980). To capture the impact of seasonality on female activities and also on disease patterns, the same households were interviewed three times - during two peak and one slack agricultural season. The details of the study design have been given in Khan (1980).

Some Observations

Even though the detailed findings of the study are not yet available, the experience from India shows that such integration is extremely rewarding and provides much more information, particularly on the dynamics of decision-making processes at the family level than could otherwise be obtained through surveys.

For example, in developing countries, most surveys show that there is a sizeable proportion of couples who do not want additional children but are yet not practising family planning. How to meet this "unmet need" is a problem, particularly if the providers of the services are not sure about the major reasons for non-acceptance of contraceptives by these potential users. The present study helps identify many of these gaps. While through the survey we were able to identify the characteristics and proportion of these couples in the general population, case studies helped us in answering the question "why do they not accept family planning?" The study shows how the women in rural areas were keen for contraception but the inaccessibility of correct family planning information and services forced them to accept unwanted children or resort to indigenous methods of abortion (Khan, Dastidar and Bairathi, 1983).

The usefulness of this approach is now being appreciated by the policy makers and research institutions like the Indian Council of Medical Research (ICMR), National Institute of Health and Family Welfare (NIHFW), Operations Research Group (ORG), India Space Research Organisation (ISRO), etc. Ministries such as the Ministry of Health and Family Welfare, the Central Statistical Organisation (CSO), etc. are also advocating its usefulness in obtaining policy relevant data. In fact many of these institutions have already initiated studies using this approach. For example, the Operations Research Group has successfully used this approach in a major study on the reasons for the under-utilisation of health and family planning services provided by the government in rural India (Khan and Prasad, 1982). In yet another study funded by ICMR, five national institutions are using this approach to collect data on the extent of illegal abortions in rural India and its consequences to health. Similarly the Ministry of Health and Family Welfare, Government of India has recently organised two national workshops to debate how to generate useful qualitative data to complement survey findings and improve and monitor the family planning programme.

However, it may be pointed out that while the integration of the two approaches is welcome and acceptable to the policy-makers, findings of only case studies are not very useful for them for policy decisions. Smallness of the sample size always reminds them that the findings cannot be generalised and hence cannot be used for broad policy issues.

Among the two components of this approach, case studies are more difficult to conduct and need careful planning and continuous monitoring right from the beginning. The following paragraphs highlight our problems and how they were solved.

a.   Need for dedicated workers

Case studies demand strong organisational support and dedicated social scientists who are ready to live in villages/ communities for extended periods of time. Getting such persons, particularly women, is difficult. During our study, many female workers joined and left. This caused many operational problems and delayed the study as each girl had to establish rapport afresh. Thus in such research it is perhaps useful to involve students who are aspiring for Ph.D. degrees in social science and allow them to use a part of the data for their own use.

b.   Maintaining interest of the informants in the study

Holding the interest of the informants for an extended period of time was yet another major problem. They did not appreciate our frequent visits to their families and answering every fifteenth day questions on how "yesterday time" was spent. Many of them felt this exercise was boring and a waste of time. To keep their interest alive, we gave small gifts to their children but we observed that in this process they became demanding. Over the period we learnt that instead of gifts, if some social work which may benefit the community (not necessarily only the informant family) is done, it increases the credibility and acceptability of the investigator. For example, one of our field workers helped many families in the village in getting flush toilets under a government development programme. She also informed the villagers about the possibility of getting loans for setting up household industries and at times helped in completing the forms. Sometimes she also assisted villages in getting treatment from government clinics or in getting domestic water connections. Even though many times such help was not rendered to the main informant families, the overall impact was very encouraging and she never faced problems in getting the required information for our study. In fact, because of these social services (which did not take much of her time), she was able to remove the apathetic attitude of the people towards the study. For example, one old man of the village had commented orginally:

It is okay: you have been given duties to fill your pages, please do it. I will answer what I can but do not fool us by saying that your study is or would ever benefit us.

But because of the social work done by the investigator, the attitude of the villagers towards the study and the investigator herself changed.

c.   Duration of stay in the village

Our experience shows that in such studies, the investigator need not stay in the village for one full year. At times it proves counter-productive. For example, the investigator who stays all the time in a village may start mixing with certain selected families and the villagers may start identifying her with a particular caste/class group. In Indian villages, which are full of caste and class conflicts, creation of such an impression could damage the study as she might not be acceptable to the other groups. Our experience shows that only at the initial stages need the investigator live in the village continuously for two-three months in order to establish rapport with the informants and their family members. Once this rapport has been established, the investigator can pull out and visit the village periodically say for 10-15 days every month to collect the relevant data.

d. Observance of village social norms

We found that for the investigator it was extremely necessary to observe the social norm while mixing with the low caste people or persons of the opposite sex. For example, accepting food or drink in Jatav or Mehtar (sweeper) families who belong to the scheduled caste group was totally taboo in the village. We initially did not observe this custom and at times accepted their hospitality. This annoyed the high caste group and we faced serious problems in getting their co-operation. In no time, we "learned" the norm and corrected our "behaviour". As a result, we stopped visiting houses of scheduled caste and other low caste families. Instead, we had to look for an opportunity to talk to them whenever we met them working at other high caste respondent families or doing personal work like fetching water from the well, fodder from the field or while visiting the nearest town for shopping.

e. Misleading answers

It was found that in the beginning the informants gave wrong answers to the questions on sensitive issues like family planning, husband-wife communication on family size, desire of additional children, etc. Later on when intimate rapport was developed, they corrected their answers. Many of them, themselves came forward for such corrections. For example, apathy of husbands towards family planning was reported only at the end of our study. When asked why they gave wrong information at first, they replied "would you tell everything about your family to a stranger on the first day without knowing his/her motives".

f. Problems in collecting of time use data

The most serious problem was the lack of a concept of time among the informants. Their concept of "one hour" varied from one person to another. Hence to understand the accuracy of the reported data on time use, observations were made in each of the sample households during a day. The families were then revisited the following day and interviewed for "yesterday time". This information when compared with the observed data, yielded a good insight into the errors involved in the reporting of time use. It helped in capturing the phenomenon of dual activities which were often performed but neglected by the respondents during interviews.

Now when we are almost completing the study, our experience says that in developing countries like India, getting accurate time use data is difficult no matter how it is collected. The estimated time of each activity should not be taken at its face value, rather it should be take as a crude approximation indicating which activity consumes relatively more time. In one of our recent studies, instead of asking the respondent exactly how much time did he/she spend on various activities, we have asked whether they spent " small amount of time", "less than half a day", "about half a day", "more than half a day", "about a full day" or "all day" on a given activity. Our hunch is that estimation of time allocation by this procedure would not be too different from the estimates based on the "exact amount of time dispensed" on various activities as reported by the respondents. If this experiment is successful, we feel collection of time allocation data, particularly from rural masses, will become much easier.

Bibliography

Anker, R. 1980. *Research on women's roles and demographic change: Survey questionnaires of households, women and men and communities with background explanations.* Geneva, ILO.

---. 1982. "Demographic change and the role of women: A research programme in developing countries", in Anker, R.; Buvinic M.; Youssef, N. (eds.): *Interactions between women's roles and population trends in the Third World.* London, Croom Helm.

Khan, M.E. 1980. *Study of inter-relationships between status of women and demographic change in Uttar Pradesh, India: A proposal*, Working Paper no. 1. New Delhi, Operations Research Group.

Khan, M.E.; Dastidar, G.; Bairathi, S. 1983. *Not wanting children yet not practising family planning: A qualitative assessment*, Working Paper no. 32. Baroda, Operations Research Group.

Khan, M.E.; Prasad, C.V.S. 1984. *Reasons for under-utilization of health service: A comparative study of the status of Bihar, Gujarat and Kerala.* Baroda, Operations Research Group.

Nag, M.; Anker, R.; Khan, M.E. 1982. *A guide to anthropological study of women's roles and demographic change in India.* Geneva, ILO; mimeographed World Employment Programme research working paper.

3.   Mauritius: Women, Factory Employment and Fertility
      - Catherine Hein
      Paper reported in Section III.3

In many Third World countries, available data suggest that urban women often have greater difficulty finding salaried employment than men.   Even in countries where women have been traditionally active outside the home, they are said to be excluded from many occupations in the "modern" sector, particularly those in industry.   The case of Mauritius presents a contrast to this situation.   In a country where female activity rates outside the home have been traditionally low, export-oriented industrialisation in the 1970s has been characterised by an almost exclusive use of female labour.

The existence of a predominantly female labour force in export-oriented assembly industries in developing counries is far from unique to Mauritius and can be found in such diverse settings as Malaysia, Mexico, Puerto Rico, South Korea and Tunisia.   The factors responsible for the high proportion of female workers as found in Mauritius may thus also apply elsewhere.

Industrialisation in Mauritius, a small island country, whose main economic activity has been sugar cane production, developed rapidly with the creation in 1970 of Export Processing Zones (EPZ).   The encouragement of labour intensive industries which produce for export was seen as one way of creating productive employment for the many unemployed.   By 1980, there were about 100 EPZ factories operating in various parts of the island, employing 22,000 people.   This constituted about 11 per cent of all employment in the formal sector (i.e. establishments employing 10 or more people).   Throughout the 1970s about 80 per cent of EPZ employment has been female.

Research was undertaken to understand the reasons for the high proportion of women in factory work in Mauritius both from the supply and the demand side of the labour market.   The results of this research are published in ILO working paper no. 114.   In addition, the possible relationship of this employment of women to fertility-related variables, such as age of marriage and use of family planning, was investigated and reported in ILO working paper no. 118.   The current paper summarises some of the main findings without going into the details.   It is divided into three sections: first, the reasons why employers prefer female rather than male workers;   secondly, the reasons why women have gone to work in the factories;   and thirdly, the relationship between women's factory employment and their fertility-related behaviour.

a.   Reasons why employers prefer women

The creation of export processing zones in developing countries is generally based on the relatively low cost of labour in that country. The industries established tend to be ones where labour is an important part of total costs such as knitting and electronics assembly. Thus, if female labour is cheaper than male and just as suitable, employers will tend to prefer women.

Indeed, interviews with employers in Mauritius indicated that a key reason for employing women was their lower minimum wage. (Twenty-three employers were interviewed employing about one-third of the industrial labour force.) As legislated by the Government, minimum wages for women are approximately three-fifths of the male minimum. Although most women workers earned more than the female minimum only about one-fifth earned more than the male minimum. Thus employers were using women for as many jobs as possible.

Not only were women cheaper, but employers considered them to be more productive than men for various reasons. For many of the jobs in the manufacture of clothing and in the electronics industry, the supposed greater manual dexterity of women was considered an asset. Employers also felt that women were more reliable and less absent than men. Indeed a few experiences with male workers tended to show that they were not only less reliable but much more troublesome and more difficult to control than women. Thus, even if minimum wages were made the same for men and women, it is likely that a high proportion of EPZ employers would continue to employ women.

In the literature which deals with women's exclusion from modern industry, the main reasons suggested for employers' preference for men are that women (a) are more absent, (b) cannot work on the machines, (c) do not have the necessary educational level, (d) cannot work at night, and (e) must be paid maternity leave. As just seen, absenteeism is deemed to be lower among women who are also considered very suited for the machines currently in use. Furthermore, the relatively high level of education of both men and women in Mauritius (e.g. in 1972, only 18 per cent of women age 20-24 had never been to school) has meant that education is not a barrier.

As concerns the night shift, although in Mauritius, the law permits women to work at night in EPZ factories (incidentally, in contradiction to ILO Convention No. 89 of 1948), in fact few have been willing to do so. This has meant that factories which wanted to have a night shift have concentrated male labour on this difficult shift and the many problems encountered have been attributed to the sex of the workers rather than the timing of their work. Thus women's refusal to work at night has been to their short-term advantage but with the inevitable greater auto-matisation of factories and the resulting necessity for 24-hour operation, continued refusal to do night work would work to their disadvantage.

With regard to maternity leave, all women employees in industry in Mauritius have the right to two months on full pay at employer cost for their first three children. However, this provision has not been a disincentive for employing women since despite this additional cost, female labour is still cheaper than male. In any case, about three-quarters of the workers were single and did not use this benefit. Indeed, they often resigned on marriage. And even among married workers, confinements were not frequent.

Thus the main factors discouraging employers from hiring women in other contexts have not been important in Mauritius. On the contrary, women were cheaper than men and perceived by employers to be more rather than less productive.

b.   Reasons why women accepted work in factories

Why are women attracted to industrial work? To answer this question, it is important to know who are the women who work in the factories and what are their possible alternative activities. A two stage stratified random sample of 380 workers in 10 factories was interviewed.

It was found that most of the women working in factories were under 25 years (about two-fifths were less than age 20) and single. Almost three-fifths of the workers had at least completed primary schooling. In Mauritius, young women did not traditionally take up employment prior to marriage despite the fact that the median marriage age in the 1970s was about 21-22 years. Thus much of the employment created in industry has gone to a new group entering the labour force who in the absence of these job opportunities would probably not have worked nor registered as unemployed.

For most single workers, factory employment is seen as temporary and many quit upon marriage, even before they are pregnant. The ideal that married women's place is in the home was found to be very strong. Even if a women would like to continue after marriage, there is often pressure from her husband to stop.

Before the creation of the EPZ, young single women with primary education could only find jobs as domestic servants or field labourers in tea or sugar plantations since they were not sufficiently educated for white-collar work. However, the factory jobs that became available were better paid than domestic service and their status and working conditions were perceived to be much better than either domestic service or field labour. Workers were attracted mainly by the possibility of earning money, in particular money for their families. Even single workers gave on average about half of their earnings to their mothers.

A further attraction of factory work was that it was more interesting than the alternative of staying at home helping with household chores. Also, in a small society where women's activities are closely supervised, it provided an opportunity to escape legitimately this family surveillance for at least part of the day. It is interesting to note that outside the factory, workers' social activities were still very much limited to family functions and there was rarely any socialising with factory acquaintances.

Thus, it is understandable that young women with few alternative employment opportunities and who often regard working as a temporary stage prior to marriage, accepted to work for lower wages than men. Employers ensured that the same types of jobs were not occupied concurrently by both men and women so there could be no direct comparison and in fact, women did not use the higher men's wages as a reference point for evaluating their own.

The Mauritian practice of setting lower minimum wages for women than men in both industry and agriculture is in obvious conflict with the ILO Convention No. 100 of 1951 of equal pay for work of equal value. What is interesting is the lack of any pressure from within the society to change this practice. It has never been an issue in recent political campaigns or in the press. No trade union has ever suggested abandoning the sex differential, nor has any women's group challenged this practice.

c.   Factory employment and fertility

The high participation of women in factory work in Mauritius provides an opportunity for testing the hypothesis that women's employment outside the home will tend to lower their fertility. This decrease would occur because:

(i)   working would tend to delay marriage
(ii)   once married, workers would tend to delay the birth of their first child
(iii)   workers would tend to have fewer children than non-working women because of role conflict between working and motherhood
(iv)   workers would be more likely to use family planning in order to obtain the goals suggested in (ii) and (iii).

These hypotheses were investigated by comparing women who worked prior to marriage and continued working afterwards with a similar group who stopped work at marriage and another control group of married women who had never worked. Groups were matched on educational level, religion and duration of marriage in order to eliminate the influence of these variables which are linked to both employment and fertility.

As concerns marriage age, women who worked in a factory prior to marriage had married at the same age as the similar women who had never worked (about 21-22 years). In some cases working may have delayed marriage but in others it precipitated it. Marriage requires money for the trousseau and for the reception. By working, some girls had been able to marry sooner than if they waited for their family to provide the money. Also, in some cases, where female workers had married later than other women, it appeared that later marriage was the cause of their working rather than the result. Thus the hypothesis that working tends to delay marriage was not supported for Mauritian factory workers.

As concerns the timing of the first child, there was no tendency for women who continued working after marriage to delay this birth. All groups of women had given birth to their first child about 16 months after marriage on average.

There was a strong tendency to delay the birth of a second child but this was not related to whether the woman was working or not. The average number of children in all three groups was just over one (1.2). The ideal gap between the first and second child was about 4 years. For most women, the second child was planned to be the last and ideal family size was on average just over two children. Women who were working did not have a lower ideal family size than those who were not.

Use of contraception, mainly the pill, was common in all groups of women. Working women were somewhat more likely to have used contraception than those not currently working - 96 per cent compared to 80 per cent. However, inactive women tended to breastfeed for longer (four months as compared to two) and about 10 per cent were still breastfeeding. Breast-feeding beyond two months was difficult for working women unless they lived within short walking distance of the factory and could return home at lunch. Thus the somewhat greater frequency of contraceptive use among workers may reflect the fact that they stop breastfeeding earlier.

The lack of evidence for the expected link between factory employment and fertility puts in question the assumption that increasing work opportunities outside the home for women will influence marriage and child-bearing patterns. Some factors which may help explain these results are:

(i)   Education, social class and marriage duration were controlled which has often not been the case in other studies.

(ii)   Fertility norms were already low and use of family planning already common in Mauritius.

(iii)   Married women who worked were a small minority for whom factory employment did not interfere with motherhood (mainly because they had a mother or mother-in-law available for child-care). In general, these two roles were incompatible and the mother role took precedence.

(iv)   A number of the working women in the study had little or no commitment to their worker role. Commit-ment of workers (or the desire to continue working) was found to be related to longer use of contra-ception, use of more reliable methods and fewer children. This suggests that it is not working per se which is related to lower fertility but commitment to working as more than a temporary stage in one's life.

The difficulties in combining factory work with motherhood are an important constraint on the supply of married women available for factory work but do not mean that married women who work tend to have fewer children. What is important is to reduce incompatibilities by such measures as increased child-care facilities and part-time employment so that mothers wishing to work can do so. Also the image of women as "secondary workers" and not "breadwinners" needs to be combatted within the society and in particular among employers, unions and women workers themselves in order that women's position in the labour market and their commitment to working may be more similar to men's.

4.   Case Studies of Women's Roles, Fertility and Family
      Planning in High Fertility Countries: Ghana and Nigeria
      - Christine Oppong
      Paper reported in Section IV.1

Introduction

West Africa has at present the highest average annual
growth rate of population of any region in the world (3.2) and
one which according to current estimates is rising, not declining.
Within the region the most populous country, Nigeria, is also the
one now growing at the fastest annual rate (3.4).   The rate of
growth of Ghana is estimated at 3.2.   Fertility rates for the
region which contribute to this growth rate are also among the
highest in the world.   The average number of children born to a
woman in her lifetime is close to seven in most countries.
Typically West African women bear their first child in their teens
and continue to bear and breastfeed children until their mid-
forties using still current traditions of post-partum abstinence to
space births.   Nearly all women are or have been wives for
much of their lives, often in polygynous marriages.   At the same
time virtually all West African women are engaged in income
generation of some kind, mostly agriculture and trade.   They
are observed to work longer hours and engage in more physical
labour than men, including gathering and transporting of fuel
and   water,   trade   and   food   production,   processing   and
preparation.
        In this paper we shall call attention to several of the small-
scale studies which have been carried out within the scope of
the ILO programme;   studies which relate to women's roles
especially the occupational and their reproductive roles. (Several
of these studies are due to be published soon in an edited
volume on Sex roles, population and development in West Africa:
research and policy issues.)   In each case the implications for
data collection and analysis, policy formulation and action programmes is spelt out.   But first, we give a short sketch of the
country contexts in which the studies were carried out.

Country contexts

Numerous   now   classic   ethnographies   of   agricultural
communities and households in both countries have documented in
great detail the traditional cultural and socio-economic contexts
of such high fertility.   They have indicated the high demand for
agricultural and domestic labour in subsistence economies with
primitive production techniques, the general availability of land
for farming in relatively sparsely populated areas and the high
levels of infant and child mortality and general vulnerability to
tropical diseases in communities with limited access to modern
medical   care,   all   of   which   have   facilitated   and   encouraged
repeated and prolonged child-bearing and begetting.   In addition,

the proximity and solidarity of kin and practices of fostering have traditionally assured the availability of multiple parental figures, who may both share the responsibilities of child-care and enjoy the benefits of children's services.

During the past two decades, demographic enquiries in both countries have noted increasing contrasts in fertility between different categories of the population by employment status, ethnicity, income level, educational standard and size of community of residence. Many tabular analyses of fertility have been undertaken documenting these differences, showing for example that farmers have more children than the rest and that the higher educated have relatively fewer children and that by and large urban/rural differences exist. In the case of South-western Nigeria, Farooq et al. (forthcoming) have recently provided an analysis of the way in which higher educational level appears to be related to lower family size preferences, as is knowledge and use of contraceptive practices.

However, contrasts between particular categories by education, employment, residence, etc. are not always those expected and West African demographers have openly admitted the difficulties involved in providing explanations for such differences. Simple one factor explanations of differences are recognised as inadequate. Moreover, they tell nothing about the causes, processes and consequences of change.

A difference which remains quite clear is that between people farming, who have on average 6-7 children and people employed in the organised sector of work separate from the home. The latter have the lowest fertility (an average of 3-4 children). Among both of these categories, however, there is considerable variation and included among the high fertility category are women self-employed and with employees and family workers, who trade as well as farm.

The diversity and change in the reproductive behaviour of the educated and employed mainly in urban settings in Ghana has been the focus of concern in a series of micro-demographic studies using a variety of materials for analysis. This work has recently been summarised, and the implications for future research underlined, in terms of concepts and methods of data collection and analysis (Oppong, 1982b). Various types of data sets from several different populations support a variety of hypotheses linking lower fertility desires and increased regu-lation of family size with increasing individualism, growing equality of parents and children, wives and husbands and increasingly flexible divisions of tasks, responsibilities and power between spouses. (See the recent review in Oppong, 1982c).

We shall now turn to the examination of a number of small scale, in-depth studies of selected groups and issues in these two country populations. Each of them has implications for various policy formulations and action.

Case study 1:   Yoruba women in a maize storage co-operative

The first case by Patricia Ladipo deals with the experiences and perceptions of a group of Nigerian rural women in a high fertility agricultural context;   a setting in which virtually all women as well as men work diligently to produce food and money to support themselves and their dependent children and parents if necessary.   Objectives of the study included identification of several types of help Yoruba women co-operative members need. Observations during the study included documenting what happens when minimal assistance of various kinds is made available to women through their co-operatives.   By the end of the project knowledge of practical use had been gained for the design of women's programmes - especially useful for demonstrating to government policy makers who set the regulations regarding co-operative support measures, that women's groups like the one studied are worth helping.

The study was carried out in an area near Ife where the introduction of maize as a cash crop and the subsequent marketing of maize by men instead of women, who traditionally marketed food crops, had led to disruption of the women's trade cycles and later to the setting up of pre-cooperative groups. Such groups were observed to assist the women to improve their skills and to increase trading capital.   However even the most progressive of these groups had not yet been granted government recognition and assistance.

Prior experience with the women in the area had indicated that there were several kinds of assistance which they wanted and needed as both workers and mothers.   These included improved technology, access to modern credit facilities and more information about childbirth and family size.

There were thus three action oriented, experimental aspects of the project, combining interventions with documentation. These included assistance to build an improved type of crib for storing and drying maize prior to sale, provision of credit and family planning information.   Remarks made by women prior to the project had indicated that women's interest in controlling their child-bearing might be stimulated by opportunities to enhance their income earning potential, as well as the impact at the farm level of other changes taking place.   The latter included the diminution of child labour through schooling, the lack of farm labour because of the urban labour demands, inflation and food shortages and development programmes which undermine women's ability to contribute to family income (e.g. the introduction of maize as a cash crop to men), as well as better communication and wider experience which increase awareness of higher levels of living.   There were signs that women's perceptions of their maternal role were changing as other changes occurred.   There was among some, an increasing concern for quality of child-care and opportunities for education available.

The provision of credit and the monitoring of its use was partly to demonstrate to government that women could handle it.

The modest amounts of money were loaned to 25 women and attempts made to interview them every two weeks.

Conclusions of the study were that the co-operative group was a suitable institution through which trading capital could be made available to women. The maize crib experiment showed that the group had a high potential for joint effort and investment. The family planning lecture was well accepted but subsequent action or adoption of modern contraception was hindered by several factors. These included lack of access to contraceptives at a price the women could afford and continuing anxieties about child mortality in a context in which half or so pregnancies end in death. Moreover male opinion and influence and women's lack of resources were inhibiting factors.

Case 2: Teenage pregnancies and school dropouts: the relevance of family life education and vocational training to girls' employment opportunities

The next case by Felix Akuffo (forthcoming), a Ghanaian social scientist, is about teenage girls in West Africa, who frequently drop out of school because they get pregnant. He studied the plight of a sample of 125 girls who dropped out of school before completing their primary courses. The main cause of leaving early was pregnancy.

This is in a context in which women are expected to work in agriculture, trade and crafts and professions and do so but where in spite of apparently equal opportunities, far fewer girls attend school at all levels, especially the higher levels, than boys. They are thus at a disadvantage in the labour market.

Another reason causing girls to leave school early is financial. Their parents are unable to continue supporting them and they seek income sources through trading and crafts. The need for financial support is often a reason for girls entering liasons with men while still in school.

The researcher remarks that the girls' access to relevant knowledge to help them pursue both income-generating opportunities and planned motherhood is minimal or non-existent. The girls lack both vocational training and family life education and yet as he remarks teachers, parents and girls are eager that training and knowledge in these areas should be expanded to help girls cope with the demand of adolescence and adulthood. Given the inability of parents to cope with their growing children's material needs and financial demands, possibilities for part-time work and schooling need to be further explored.

Case 3: Ghanaian educated women: Sixty focused biographies

The next case is one concerning the analysis of 60 focused biographies of educated Ghanaian women from two ethnic groups living in two different towns and among whom are migrants and locals, and younger and older women (Oppong and Abu, 1984). An aim of this study was to discover some of the reasons why a set of women living in a highly pronatalist region want and get fewer children than their contemporaries. It focuses upon the multiple interactions between their several roles, in particular their occupational role and their maternal activities of child-bearing and rearing.

It explores in detail possible role conflicts and role strains caused by lack of time or money, as well as innovative role expectations which might be associated with changing family size desires or contraceptive practice. Different kinds of employment and income generation and migration away from kin and educational levels are seen to have multiple effects upon various roles, both behaviour and expectations. Some of these have the ultimate outcome of making motherhood more a cause of expense, ambition, emotional investment, individual concern and problems. These changes in turn can be linked to a desire for fewer children of higher quality, in terms of education and parental investment (maternal resources, time and interest).

A conclusion of the study is that changes in the maternal role involving greater stress on modern approaches to child-care and child quality associated with desires for fewer children are also linked with changing elements in other roles: greater concern for community life and participation in it, involvement in status enhancing jobs, greater flexibility and emotional salience in marriage and higher levels of living within the home.

At the same time more systematic contraceptive use is associated with more individualised mothering, looser links with kin, a more active individual role (with peers, friends et al.) and an occupation which calls for longer hours of work away from home causing perceptions of time strain and greater conflict between occupational and domestic activities.

These findings from 60 detailed biographies provide insights into the kinds of changes in role systems linking new educational opportunities and occupations and the associated migration with reproductive change.

Case 4:   Responsible fatherhood and birth planning

The last case study we shall mention here was actually a study of men as fathers, including their family size desires and contraceptive practices (Oppong, 1983). The men were Ghanaian teachers and aspects of their relationships with their wives, kin and children were examined to see how these appeared to be related to reproductive goals and behaviour.

This study is quite pertinent to our concerns here for it underlines a number of ways in which changes in relationships between women and men as spouses in marriage and as parents and children are related to demographic innovation. Several of the relevant findings were that family size desires were likely to be lower and contraceptive use more consistent: (1) the more relationships in marriage were flexible and egalitarian (2) the more fathers assumed individual responsibility for their offspring rather than indulging in traditional practices of fostering of children by kin and (3) the more they had the same aspirations for their daughters' education as for their sons. In other words aspects of sexual equality in the domestic domain and individual responsibility were linked to demographic innovation. In addition the greater equality of wives was in turn associated with their levels of education, occupations and material support for family members. Equality within the home was linked to equality in occupational life.

Policy implications

In the co-operative study in Southern Nigeria, the author noted that the findings pointed to the need to review the government's co-operative registration policy and the need to grant recognition to groups showing an acceptable growth rate. Access to loans and information through co-operative membership might enhance women's income sufficiently for them to have more ability to cope with family demands and provide for health needs, as well as enhancing the desire to control their fertility. The study underlined the need for available and appropriate contraception and health care facilities.

Once more the appropriateness of using women's work groups for dissemination of information about family size and planning was vividly illustrated and the author also pointed to the potential use of such groups for affecting the knowledge and behaviour of the women's teenage children among whom pregnancy before establishment of marriage and an occupation was becoming a problem.

The study on schoolgirl mothers underlined the intrinsic need to combine vocational training with family welfare and planning education - a need which has been recognised by the Ghana National Council of Women and Development (GNCWD). At the same time it gives evidence to support the contention made by Bleek (forthcoming) that more attention should be given to the young in realistic family welfare and planning programmes - those who are least equipped to face the heavy responsibilities of sudden and unplanned parenthood.

The third case had important research implications, indicating the need to look in more detail at the ways in which roles and their attached activities, resources, responsibilities and goals harmonise or conflict if we are to understand pressures towards innovation at the individual level. A practical concern which also emerged during the course of the study was women's need to know more about the potential ill-effects of illegal abortion and different contraceptive methods and their possible effects.

The fourth study mentioned added more evidence to the contention that sexual equality in the market place and home and shouldering of individual parental responsibilities are linked to smaller family size and family planning. It also emphasised the need for more knowledge about men's roles as parents, if greater understanding is to be gained of reproduction and socialisation and how and why these may be changing in different social and cultural contexts.

Thus each of these small case studies in its own modest way helped to throw more light on problems and needs of women in a high fertility, high economic participation area. At the same time they served to underline, at minimum research cost, the importance of putting into effect certain policies and programmes affecting women, their employment and fertility. In addition they serve to throw more light on contemporary issues of social change in countries in which national data sets at the present time are largely lacking, and even where available, tell us little about the dynamic processes of change.

References

Akuffo, F.O. Forthcoming. "Teenage pregnancies and school dropouts: The relevance of family life education and vocational training to girls' employment opportunities", in C. Oppong (ed.): Forthcoming.

Bleek, W. Forthcoming. "Family and family planning in Southern Ghana", in C. Oppong (ed.): Forthcoming.

Farooq, G.; Ekanem, I.; Ojelade, M.A. Forthcoming. "Family size preferences and fertility in South Western Nigeria" in C. Oppong (ed.): Forthcoming.

Oppong, C. 1982a. *Maternal role rewards, opportunity costs and fertility*. Geneva, ILO; mimeographed World Employment Programme research working paper.

---. 1982b. *Reproduction and resources: Some anthropological evidence from Ghana*. Geneva, ILO; mimeographed World Employment Programme research working paper.

---. 1982c. *Familial roles and fertility: Some labour policy aspects*. Geneva, ILO; mimeographed World Employment Programme research working paper.

---. 1983. *Paternal costs, role strain and fertility regulation: Some Ghanaian evidence*. Geneva, ILO; mimeographed World Employment Programme research working paper.

Oppong, C.; Abu, K. 1984. *The changing maternal role of Ghanaian women: Education, migration and employment*. Geneva, ILO; mimeographed World Employment Programme research working paper.

---. (ed.) Forthcoming. *Sex roles, population and development in West Africa: research and policy issues*. Geneva, ILO.

Orubuloye, I. Forthcoming. "Values and costs of daughters and sons to Yoruba mothers and fathers", in C. Oppong (ed.): Forthcoming.

Pittin, R. 1982. *Documentation of women's work in Nigeria: Problems and solutions*. Geneva, ILO; mimeographed World Employment Programme research working paper.

Ware, M. 1983. "Female and male life cycles", in C. Oppong (ed.): *Female and male in West Africa*. London, George Allen and Unwin.

5.   The Demographic Transition in Cuba: Women's economic
      and social roles
      - Alfonso Farnos and Celestino Alvarez-Lajonchere
      Reported in Section IV.2

a.   Some aspects of the demographic situation

The political, economic and social transformations that took place in Cuba after the triumph of the Revolution in 1959 have been reflected in the levels and tendencies of demographic growth. Currently, Cuba is passing through what we could call the last phase of the demographic transition.

From the first years of the Revolution a plan for preferential attention to the health sector was drawn up. This policy has been so successful that currently average life expectancy at birth is 72 years and the infant mortality rate is only 18 deaths per thousand live births.

A marked decrease in levels of fertility has been observed since the late 1960s. Table 1 shows the rapid decline of the gross reproduction rate (GRR) to 0.87 in 1980 - a rate which is beneath the natural replacement level.

Table 1:   Cuba: Gross reproduction rate in selected
            years

Year	GRR (daughters per woman)
1970	1.80
1975	1.33
1980	0.87

Source: State Statistics Committee (SSC), 1980 and
           preliminary figures (1980).

Table 2:   Cuba: Population structure by major age
            groups from 1970 and 1981 censuses

Age	1970	1981
0-14	36.9	30.3
15-64	57.1	62.0
65 and over	6.0	7.7
Total	100.0	100.0

Source: SSC, 1983

Current fertility levels are similar to those in many developed countries and even lower than in other socialist countries (see figure 1). The effects of declining fertility are reflected in the age structure of the population.

Figure 1: Total fertility rates in selected socialist countries, 1971-81

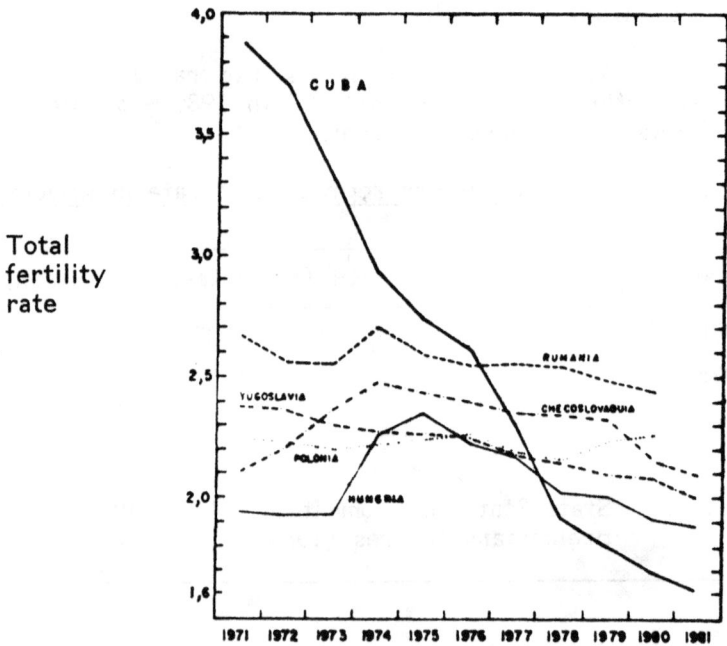

Source: State Statistics Committee, 1982.

In this demographic process there are some tendencies which should be studied more deeply. The fertility structure has become younger. Younger women have increased their relative contribution to fertility and women above age 30 have decreased considerably their participation in the reproductive process. Figure 2 shows the age specific fertility rates through this century. The recent rapid decline of fertility in all age groups is evident although the decline is less among 15-19 year olds.

Figure 2: Age specific fertility rates in Cuba, 1907-1975

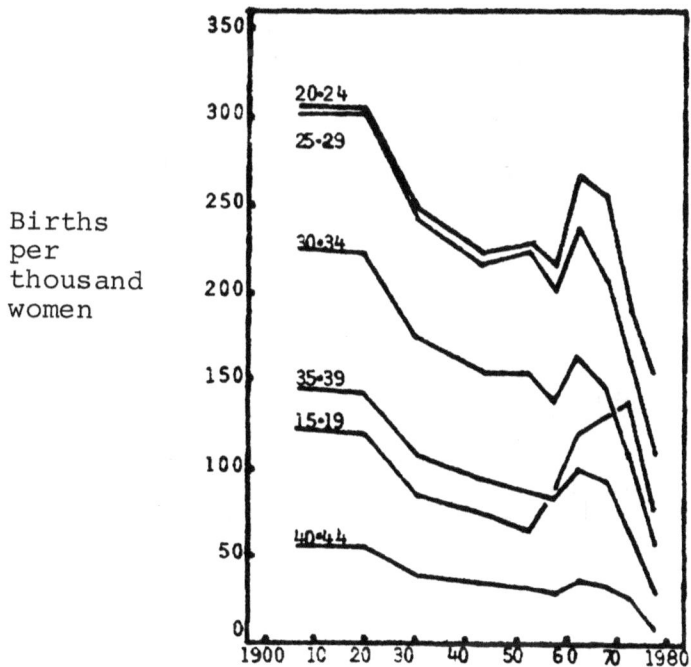

Source: SSC and CELADE (1981)

Table 3: Cuba: Percentage distribution of the age specific
fertility rates, 1970, 1975 and 1982

Ages	1970	1975	1982
15-19	17.3	21.4	25.8
20-24	30.9	32.0	34.1
25-29	22.2	21.8	22.3
30-34	15.4	13.8	11.7
35-39	10.0	7.7	4.6
40-44	3.6	2.9	1.3
45-49	0.6	0.4	0.2
Total	100.0	100.0	100.0

Source: SSC, 1980 and preliminary figures (1982).

Table 4: Percentage distribution of marital status
for persons aged 14 years and above,
1970 and 1981

Conjugal situation	1970	1981
Unmarried	30.7	28.5
Married	40.3	41.5
Living together	21.3	20.4
Divorced	3.3	5.1
Widowed	4.4	4.5
Total	100.0	100.0

Source: SSC, 1983

Another aspect that attracts attention is related to marriage and divorce. If we take data from the last censuses, we observe that the group "divorced" has increased while the proportion of persons "married or living together" is fairly stable. Furthermore, the phenomenon of early marriages is an element which should be studied.

b.   The women's economic and social roles

In the new Cuban society, women's economic participation has gained importance. From a dependent capitalist society, the country changed to the construction of a socialist society.

In this process, the role of women has been transformed. The general cultural level of the population and particularly of women has increased as well as participation in productive activity. The liberation from the conjugal chains existing before is also an element which has influenced the country's demographic process.

In order to have a general idea of the results of women's incorporation into social life some interesting data can be found in the September 1981 census.

Table 5:   Percentage distribution by sex of graduates at selected educational levels, 1981 census

Educational level	Men	Women	Total
Medium level technician	59.9	40.1	100.0
Teacher's formation	40.4	59.6	100.0
High level education	58.0	42.0	100.0

Sources: SSC 1983

In that census, 32.8 per cent of women older than fifteen years declared themselves as economically active and currently a little more than one of three working persons is a woman. Nevertheless, an important part of the female population is still not integrated into an active social life. About 47 per cent of the female population older than fifteen years was dedicated to "home work" in the 1981 census.

In 1970, 60.5 per cent of the population lived in urban areas, in 1981 it reached 69.0. In 1970 there were 17 TV sets for every 100 homes, now there are 58. There were 24 refrigerators for every 100 homes, now there are more than 50.

These data give proof of the facilities which are available to the Cuban family. On the whole, all the interrelations of the economic and social factors contribute to slowly change the role played by women in society.

c.   Research on women's role and demographic change in Cuba

A research project was set up by the Cuban Women's Federation and the Demographic Research Centre of Havana University and is being finished with the help of the International Labour Organisation.

This research has been named "Women's role and the demographic changes in Cuba". In it, three areas of the country have been studied comparatively: the most urban municipality existing in the capital - Place of the Revolution; a semi-urban area in the central zone of the country - Buenavista; and the most rural and mountainous municipality in Cuba - Yateras. Also comparisons have been made with other research. The central objective is to investigate the interrelations between the reproductive behaviour of women and their participation in economic activity. Also, studied is the interrelation between educational levels and the lowering of fertility and the differences that still exist between the urban and rural areas. Other more specific aspects like the use of contraceptives, the problems of couples, etc. have also been considered.

To carry out this research, a questionnaire was developed and administered, through sampling methods, to more than 3,000 women between the ages of 15 and 59 years in the month of September 1982, in the three above-mentioned places.

Most relevant results

It was confirmed in the research that fertility has considerably diminished during the last ten years, particularly in rural areas, where levels were higher in other times. In this way, the differences existing between urban and rural areas have diminished.

An element directly tied with this reduction is the wider use of contraceptive methods in rural areas. Research carried out in the seventies showed that contraceptives were known but not used. The rural area of this research - Yateras - has health services, education, communications and a commercial network non-existent in other times. In other words, the most rural area has become more urbanised thanks to a process of socio-economic development and, consequently, its levels of fertility have been reduced as well as the levels of mortality.

The fertility of women between 15 and 19 years of age has become important. Early childbearing can involve risks to the health of mother and child. Furthermore, a baby conceived without adequate physical and psychological maturity can bring about other effects after the birth of the baby: limitations on the educational, cultural and active life of the mother, rupture of friendships, inadequate attention to the child, etc. We need to investigate the causes of conjugal unions and births at an early age. The results of the survey show that there is a high proportion of divorced women in the more urbanised area. The woman's economic independence is an important element in this case. With a higher educational level we can observe generally a greater stability in marriages. But, the results show that more than 25 per cent of the surveyed women have been married at least twice. This aspect requires additional research.

Abortion plays an important role in birth control and its incidence is higher in the analysed urban area than in the rural one. There exists a policy aimed at educating the people to use contraceptive methods rather than abortion for birth control. To achieve this goal, sexual education is being given wider publicity.

In analysing the interrelation between reproductive patterns and educational levels it was observed that there is lower fertility at higher educational levels but the differences are not substantial. The fertility patterns are reaching the same levels regardless of education. Also, we must bear in mind, that the educational level is increasing in all the analysed areas.

Another important result of the research shows the high percentage of married women who declared that they were studying: 40 per cent in the more urbanised area and 37 per cent in the rural one.

There were still differences between the levels of fertility of working and non-working women at the moment when this survey was made in each of the areas. But, at the same time that the fertility levels have become lower during the past ten years, so the above mentioned differences have decreased.

It is not possible on this occasion to describe all the results. It is enough to say that in this research we also analyse reproductive ideals, spacing between births, some characteristics of the homes where women live, etc. In the above paragraphs we have mentioned the more important recommendations. Others could be related to the real possibility of increasing female participation in economic activity.

The existence of a socialist economy in the country guarantees that the bases are created in order to obtain a higher integration of women into society. Policies and directives aim in that direction. There are, however, objective questions and in other cases subjective ones that constrain female integration to a slower pace.

Bibliography

Federación de Mujeres Cubanas (FMC), Centro de Estudios Demográficos (CEDEM) [Federation of Cuban Women, Demographic Research Centre]. Unpublished. *El papel de la mujer y los cambios demograficos en Cuba* [The roles of women and demographic changes in Cuba]. Havana, FMC.

State Statistics Committee (SSC). 1980. *Proyeccion de la poblacion cubana 1950-2000 nivel nacional: Metodologia y resultados* (actualizacion en junio de 1980) [Projection of the Cuban population 1950-2000, national level: Methodology and results (brought up to date in June 1980)]. Havana, SSC.

---. 1982. *Censos de pobacion y vivienda 1981. El envejecimiento de la poblacion y los longevos residentes en Cuba* [Census of population and dwellings 1981. Aging of population and the elderly residents in Cuba]. Havana, SSC.

---. 1983. *Censos de poblacion y vivienda 1981* [Census of popuation and dwellings 1981]. Havana, SSC.

--- y Centro Latinoamericano de Demografía (CELADE). 1981. *Cuba: El descenso de la fecundidad 1964-1978* [Cuba: Fertility decline 1964-1978]. Havana, SSC.

6. The Female Employment Situation in the Soviet Union
   - Svetlana Turchaninova
   Paper reported in Section V.

When examining female employment and the character of female labour utilisation, it should be remembered that women are a highly specific category of workers. One of the specific characteristics of women as workers is the close relationship between female economic activity and the role women play in reproduction and child-rearing. This is why, in socialist society, women's work is viewed from the point of view of both purely economic interests and wider social interests, the underlying assumption being that child-bearing and rearing of physically and morally healthy children are as important to continued social progress as women's achievements in economic life.

In the Soviet Union, consistent efforts have been made to achieve genuine social and economic equality between women and men and, more specifically, to create conditions allowing women to harmoniously combine their two social functions as creators of material and cultural wealth and as mothers and educators of the younger generation.

These conditions include various social benefits, particular consideration of working women's occupational safety and health, steady improvement of working conditions, excellent vocational training and retraining opportunities, and increasing government aid to the family. Combined with the national system of protection of mothers and children, these measures help provide working women with optimal conditions for successfully combining economic activity, maternity and all-round personality development.

In the 1970s-80s, the rate of female participation in the national economy was at 90-93 per cent, 7.5 per cent being engaged in full-time studies. Since 1970, the relative share of women in the national labour force has stood at a national average of 51 per cent not going down below 40 per cent in any individual constituent republic. In the present-day stage of developed socialist society, the key problem is how to ensure the most rational employment of women and raise the efficiency of female labour.

In order to ensure the most rational employment of women in the socialist economy, the following underlying principles must be met:
- maintaining the correct balance between the employment of women in social production and in the home economy at a given stage of socio-economic development;
- adapting the character of work and conditions to the specific physical and mental characteristics of working women;
- ensuring the optimal pattern of work and rest to enable women to combine participation in social production with their maternal and other family responsibilities.

The high rate of female labour force participation is not in itself a sufficient test of rational female labour force utilisation unless it is accompanied by fertility and reproduction patterns that meet the needs of social development. This is to say that the increasing participation of women in social production, essentially a progressive process, must have its reasonable limits, taking into account the interests of women as mothers. In other words, whatever the social and economic benefits of increased participation by women in the national economy, we must consider its possible consequences for population trends.

Participation of some women of working age in the home economy is an important element in the rational female employment pattern. According to the 1970 Census, women employed in the home economy accounted for 7.5 per cent of all women of working age as against 25.4 per cent in 1959. [1]

The fact that a given number of women of working age participate in the home economy at any given time should not mean that they are excluded from the national economy once and for all. The typical Soviet woman today is not the housewife forever tied to the kitchen, but a woman actively engaged in the national economy and leaving productive work only to give birth and raise small children. Soviet economists have established that an average working woman participated in industry, agriculture or office work for a total of 28.7 years in her working life in the 1960s as against 33.5 years in the 1970s, withdrawing from social production for an average of 12.3 years in the 1960s as compared with an average of just 3.6 years in the 1970s. [2]

Among the many socio-economic and psychological causes of declining birth-rate in the Soviet Union the high level of female labour force participation is one of the more important. The greatest drop in birth-rate was registered during the 1960s because it was during that decade that large numbers of women left the home economy and the family holding to participate in social production. The natural yearly growth in population in the Soviet Union was 8.2 per 1,000 in 1980 as against 17.6 in 1960, a drop of more than one half. [3]

Beginning in the mid-1970s, greater attention was paid to the formulation and implementation of effective population policies. During the Tenth Five-Year Plan period (1976-80), a number of steps were taken to improve women's working conditions, family recreation and holidays, welfare and recreational facilities for families. The Government is introducing in 1981-83 paid maternity leave of 12 months after child-birth, followed by additional leave without pay up to the age of 18 months, to be extended to 24 months in the future, during which the child's mother retains her continuous service record as well as length of service in a given occupation.

In addition to the increased numbers of working women, substantial changes in the structure of employment and utilisation of female labour in the Soviet Union can be observed. Today, women account for just over half the labour force in the Soviet Union and their participation is high in all branches of the economy - 51 per cent of all industrial workers and office employees and 54 per cent of collective farmers, 55 per cent of all specialists, 47 per cent of all research workers, 48 per cent of all workers in industry, 29 per cent of construction workers, 63 per cent of administrative workers, 73 per cent of workers in education and recreation, 82 per cent of all workers in health, physical recreation and social security, 83 per cent of all workers in commerce and public catering.[4]

Within individual branches of the national economy, the balance between male and female labour varies considerably, depending first and foremost on working conditions and the nature of work in a given industry. Male labour dominates industries like mining, transport, construction and forestry where there are strenuous or unhealthy jobs which are barred to women under the existing labour laws. In these industries, women account for less than 30 per cent of the labour force. In the sphere of material production as a whole, female workers constitute 45 per cent of the labour force. Female labour dominates the non-productive industries taking almost 69 per cent of such employment.

In the Soviet Union today, over one-third of all working women are employed in manufacturing industries. Women account for almost half of all industrial workers, the leading social group in the USSR. Almost 70 per cent of all women working in industry are employed in engineering, consumer goods, and food industry leaving a smaller percentage of the industrial female force to other branches of manufacturing.

It is worth mentioning that the highest rate of growth in female employment has been registered not in traditional female industries like textile, garment industry or primary and secondary education, but primarily in industries connected with technological innovation and urban developments - engineering, chemical industry, scientific research, etc.

Soviet women are moving into new areas of employment, with women increasing, in particular, their share of what is known as creative occupations. Comparison of the data provided by the 1939 and 1979 national Census gives a graphic picture of the substantial re-distribution in women's share of physical and intellectual work. In 1939, manual workers accounted for 88 per cent of all women gainfully employed as compared with 65 per cent in 1979. At the same time, women's share of manual employment has remained almost unchanged at 46-47 per cent while their share of office jobs has risen from 26 to 60 per cent.[5]

Changes in the character and content of women's work can also be observed in production jobs. As a result of accelerated technological innovation, strenuous manual work is increasingly replaced by machine production and simple production jobs by skilled labour. Today, women account for nearly half the workers involved in mechanised work. The proportion of women has increased in such essentially creative occupations as adjusters, operators, machinists, fitters, metal workers, electricians, and others closely associated with technological innovation.

Increased educational and professional standards of Soviet working women are secured through compulsory secondary schooling and a network of vocational and technical schools and colleges offering general education and specialist training on both a full-time and part-time basis. Factory and office workers engaged in part-time further education programmes enjoy a wide range of benefits including shorter working week, paid leave to research the final term paper and take final examinations, educational leave following the birth of a child and more.

Over the past 20 years, the Soviet working women's educational standards have been almost the same as those of men. In 1979, out of every thousand workers of each sex, 810 men and 801 women had complete or incomplete higher or secondary education.[6] Moreover, according to the 1970 national Census, women below 35 had higher standards of education as compared with men of the same age group. Today, young women account for 57 and 52 per cent of students of technical schools and colleges respectively.[7]

However, for all the progress made by women in the field of vocational training and further training, it would be wrong to assume that all the problems have been solved. While women equal men in terms of training standards in the national economy as a whole, in some occupational groups and industries the women's levels of skill and training lag behind those of men. The main reason is the insufficient rationalisation of housework. Despite substantial progresss in developing public catering, community services and pre-school children's institutions, working women have to shoulder a large amount of family work. Women have 1.5-2 times less leisure time than men. Thus working women with little children have fewer opportunities for further vocational training which requires extra time and effort. Studies have shown that women under 30 make slower progress in vocational retraining than men of the same age group. In order to facilitate women's access to new skills, as from 1979 working mothers of young children are entitled to training on a full-time basis with average pay.

The relatively low training standards of some working women and the less advanced technology of industries with a predominantly female labour force, quite naturally, lead to the relatively low pay of working women as compared with men. However, there is no substantial difference in the pay levels of men and women in enterprises with a high level of mechanisation and automation.

The goal of rationalising the use of female labour pre-supposes a continued improvement of the system of women's vocational training and retraining which should help relieve women of the less creative and less responsible jobs involving physical effort of varying degrees of intensity. This goal will be served by the Comprehensive Mechanisation Programme aimed at reducing physical labour in different branches of the national economy as part of the National Plan of Social and Economic Development for 1981-85.

The goal of rationalising female labour force utilisation must include special measures to protect working women (such as expanding the list of unhealthy occupations and jobs barred to women, reducing the maximum weights that can be handled by women in the workplace), further benefits to working mothers (such as longer holidays, comfortable work and rest patterns, shorter working hours), improved working and welfare conditions of women workers (such as improved occupational safety and health provisions, introducing machines and equipment meeting the optimal female ergonomic standards, extending the application of shorter working hours and flexible time provisions, etc.). And, lastly the goal of rationalising the employment of women will be served by improved living conditions, higher living standards, and greater government assistance to families and individual working women in raising the younger generation.

Footnotes

[1] See *Vestnik statistiki* [Statistical abstracts], p. 80, No. 1, 1973.

[2] A.E. Kotlyar, S. Turchaninova, *Female employment in industry*, p. 1067, Moscow, 1975.

[3] L.A. Kostin, *Labour resources in the Eleventh Five-Year Plan*, p. 7-8, Moscow, 1981.

[4] *The national economy of the USSR (1922-82)*, p. 403, Moscow, 1982.

[5] E.B. Gruzdeva and E.S. Chertikhina, *Work and welfare of Soviet women*, pp. 19-20, Moscow, 1983.

[6] *National economy of the USSR in 1980*, p. 28; *Results of the 1970 All-Union Census*, p. 66, v5; *Vestnick statistiki* [Statistical Abstracts], p. 63, No. 2. 1981.

[7] *Vestnik statistiki* [Statistical abstracts], p. 74, No. 1, 1983.

7. Government Perspectives on Utilisation of Research on
    Women and Population Issues in Pakistan
    - Attiya Inayatullah
    Paper reported in Section VI.2

        Policy formulation is a function of the Planning Commission,
of which the Ministry for Planning and Development is the
administrative Ministry of the Government of Pakistan. The
major policy document is the country's Five Year Development
Plans. In preparation of these plans there is an extensive
consultation throughout the government, public and private
sectors. The placement of the Population Division in the Ministry
for Planning and Development is a clear indication of the Government's recognition of the importance of population issues in
development planning effort.
        For the purpose of this paper, research is defined within a
comprehensive perspective recognising all tools and instruments
which may provide macro or micro information on a one time
basis or over a period of time, generate data, collect statistics,
investigate phenomena, test hypotheses and assumptions.
        The usefulness of research is often contested and the
debate is neither likely to abate nor be resolved. However,
what is relevant is the government's attitude on the subject.
Who is the government? In this specific case it is the Ministry
for Planning and Development, Population Welfare Division and
Women's Division. It augurs well for Pakistan that in all three
government forums there is an implicit strong support for
"research", as well as recognition that without informed sources
and materials, the foundation or base of all efforts will be weak.
Further, population and women's sector activities have been
developed in the form of well-formulated projects, an essential
element of which is built-in monitoring and flexibility allowing a
continuing sense of exploration or search for directions that
appear to meet the purposes and objectives of policy goals.
        The gamut and range of research undertakings and
utilisation of what exists is both numerous and extensive. For
purposes of illustration a few examples are provided in the
following.
        In the history of development planning in Pakistan, for the
first time the Sixth Five Year Plan, covering the period 1983-88,
recognised clearly in its objectives and overview chapter that the
population programme in and of itself was not expected to achieve
the demographic objectives of the Plan; equally important was
the role of the development strategies. A methodology is under
preparation where through a retrieval system the stated goals of
policy objectives will be measured and correlated to expected
effects on the fertility behaviour and levels. The findings will
be periodically reviewed and recommendations made in respect of
stated policy, goals actually achieved and expected results.
From such an exercise, necessary shifts in sectoral development
strategies will be effected in order to ensure that population

issues are adequately addressed. The defined policy strategy may be a direct or indirect intervention. A simultaneous factor model is being prepared and considered for application. In a trial run, policy strategies relating to women's employment, health, education, rural electrification - and the project on special development of Baluchistan are being simulated. This important exercise is jointly undertaken by the Planning Division and Population Division.

The Population Development Centre of the Population Division has operative a client record card system which provides on a quarterly basis a critical mass of data pertaining to service performance, logistics, supply and distribution, information and education, management functions, community involvement and financial information. The data generated provide both a performance and financial audit as well as a policy monitor. As a follow-up, remedial actions are identified and taken.

The Population Development Centre has an equally strong second function which is demographic data gathering and analysis, going beyond family planning to social policy measures, research of socio-psychological and behaviour phenomena, including small-scale in-depth studies which pertain to target populations, geographic issues, area specific problems or social behaviour. Socio-demographic data from the Population Census, demographic household surveys, contraceptive use prevalence surveys, population growth studies, Pakistan fertility survey are used for review and examination of existing laws and executive orders and exploration of policy measures pertaining to incentives, interlinkage between status, role and function of women to the practice of family planning, the GAP between awareness and practice, demographic impact of the increase in age at marriage, its causes and consequences, etc.

The Population Development Centre is responsible for the research of all approaches and methodologies deployed in the population sector programme. The programme is multi-sectoral and multi-disciplinary in approach; the emergent issues are many, from the single question of the performance-related honorarium to the involvement of the traditional birth attendant, community workers, or the mammoth tasks of co-ordination between participating but competing arms of the government. The findings of the applied research are periodically fed back to the policy-maker and planner.

The National Research Institute of Fertility Control has a range of biomedical and socio-medical research in hand. It is a registered CCRC unit of WHO and ensures not only the safety and reliability of contraceptives offered but also examines their socio-cultural acceptability. They are working on "unani" (traditional) medicine and on the user perspective.

The Population Development Centre and the National Research Institute of Fertility Control are hence by and large entrusted with the task of providing the population programme with both a management monitoring system and a population information system.

The Sixth Five Year Plan document included for the first time a chapter on women's development; in addition, in recognition of the government's intent to ensure that woman is both the beneficiary and participant in the development process, a substantial financial allocation is being made for women's programmes. The Plan document gives details of women's development activities which are reflected over the twelve plan sectors.

The Women's Division, since its very inception in 1980, has had a Research Wing, the other Wing being for the programme. It is fortunate that the bias for research of a senior officer of the Women's Division made it an important and visible component in the division's activities. The results obtained are substantial because informed comment is both convincing for the planner and also provides a firm base to programmers for women, be it in the population, education or health field. Some of the important research undertaken which would be of interest to the ILO is listed as an example of the strong research perspective given to the newly founded Division:

(i)   Women in industry
(ii)   Contribution of housewives to GNP; a case study
(iii)   Patterns of female employment
(iv)   Protective legislation for factory women in Pakistan
(v)   Utilisation of human resources: the case of women in Pakistan
(vi)   Women at work, study of values of attitudes of officials about employment of women in Pakistan
(vii)   Demography, family and status of women in family laws
(viii) Men, women and work, reflections on the two-person career
(ix)   Rural women's participation in farm operations.

In 1982 a seminar entitled "Employment for Women in Pakistan" was convened in Islamabad. It is noteworthy that the policy and programmes for women were constructed following the research effort.

Pakistan's research efforts in the population and women's field are co-ordinated by the relevant divisions; however, over the years a number of research institutes have been involved in these research undertakings, such as the Pakistan Institute for Development Economics, Pakistan Women's Institute, Applied Economic Research Centre, Sind Regional Planning Organisation, Social Sciences Research Centre, Rural Development Academy, Central Statistical Organisation, Institute of Psychology, departments of universities, etc. The institutional framework for designing, organising and implementing policy and programme research appears to have been established in Pakistan.

The utilisation in Pakistan of research findings and data in the population field and on women's issues in policy formulation is abundantly clear. Policy is not a static concept; conversely, it grows and is strengthened when based on scientific data and empirical research. Some of the important questions for the Pakistan Government include:

- What is the balance between basic and applied research in Pakistan?
- How is research structured at grass-roots levels?
- What are the mechanisms for the two-way flow of information and does the policy-maker and administrator recognise the essential nature of utilising research?
- What are the mechanisms for involvement of the recipient of the programme and the planner?
- How long does it normally take for research reports to be released after completion?
- How can research findings be made less laborious and more convincing?
- Is risk money for innovative research undertaken on a pilot basis available?
- What is the level of funding for research?

Resources being limited and the serviceability and utility of research being frequently doubted, it is essential that for optimum advantage this important input be addressed with the seriousness it warrants.

8.   Information for Policy Formulation in Hungary
     - Karoly Miltenyi
     Paper reported in Section VI.2

The system of permanent communication and dialogue between policy-makers/planners and professional research workers is a general characteristic of the socialist countries. In the last two decades this system has developed also in the field of demography/population policy. This paper tries to outline:

  A. The organisational scheme and the mechanism of this
      system.
  B. The main results of the demographic research utilised
      in policy formulation.

A. The central organ for long-term planning and policy formulation is the National Planning Office. Policy formulation takes place within the framework of committees, consisting of the representatives and experts of the relevant state organs, and of social and scientific organisations.

Recognising the interdependence of demographic socio-economic, cultural, and health factors and the need for a consistent, integrated policy covering all these aspects, population policy formulation takes place within the framework of the Committee for General Long-term Planning, dealing with the following sectors:

  (i)   Population
  (ii)   Employment
  (iii)   Income and social policy
  (iv)   Consumption
  (v)   Housing
  (vi)   Health
  (vii)   Education
  (viii)   Culture

The process of policy formulation is iterative; alternative policies for each topic are first elaborated by sub-committees and then adjusted to each other in the next phase of planning; this process may be repeated.

The sub-committee for population makes extensive use of the results of demographic research. This is facilitated by the fact that the programme and especially the priorities of the scientific research are determined or, at least strongly influenced, by the requirements of the government and the policy formulating organs. Thus, for example, the programme of the Demographic Research Institute of the Hungarian Central Statistical Office is part of the general social research programme initiated by, and oriented to, policy formulation. Being the central organ for population research, the Demographic Research

Institute is responsible also for the co-ordination of the population research of other scientific bodies such as universities, research institutes for sociology, etc.

B. The main results of demographic research which have been utilised for policy formulation in the last decade can be summarised as follows.

(i)   Population projections 1983-2000

Based on the component method (i.e. indicating the expected sex/age structure), population projections are regularly revised. Revision and/or new projection is needed usually every two or three years mainly because of the changes in the fertility assumptions. Applying various fertility and mortality assumptions (generally 3-low, medium, high) alternative projections are prepared.

Population projections constitute the basis for medium and long term planning in all fields indicated in part A of this paper. For the purposes of housing and consumption policy, projections on households/ families are also needed and prepared.

(ii)   Setting the population policy targets

From the economic point of view, this target is based on the concept of the optimum dependency ratio and minimum dependency burden, elaborated by Bourgeois-Pichat and adapted to national conditions in several countries. In Hungary, research on this topic indicated that the minimum of the dependency burden can be achieved with the age structure of a stable population characterised by a net reproduction rate of 1.0-1.1. Reaching this conclusion after some discussion it was accepted in 1973 that the officially declared basic target of Hungarian policy is to ensure the simple reproduction, i.e. the net reproduction rate of 1.0.

The results of other population and medical research projects were also utilised in setting some auxiliary targets, i.e. to smooth the irregularities of the age structure, to reduce the proportion of immature babies, etc.

(iii)   Utilisation of survey results in policy formulation

Realising that effective long-term population policy can be pursued only with the co-operation and acceptance of the population, several sample surveys were conducted on this subject. Some of them were KAP (Knowledge, Attitude and Practice of Family Planning) surveys, others public opinion polls (opinions on family size and population policy). Some of the surveys were of a longitudinal, follow-up nature; they started at marriage and the couples covered were re-interviewed some years later. This offered a good opportunity to investigate the factors influencing fertility decisions and their modifications in the course of marital life. Some findings of these surveys, utilised in policy formulation can be outlined as follows.

a.   When first married, the majority of the couples indicated two children as ideal. However, a significant number stopped after the first child because of financial, housing and other problems perceived after the birth of the first child. To alleviate their difficulties, from July 1983 family allowance is given to one child families. However, the one child family allowance is paid only till the child's sixth birthday; if during these years no second child is born, the family will no longer receive family allowance.

b.   Considering the popularity of the two child family model, the original 1973 government decree, stating that it is necessary to have three children to qualify for an induced abortion, was slightly modified. In the implementation of the regulation by the Minister of Health, three children, or two children plus any additional obstetrical event such as a live birth, still-birth, induced abortion or spontaneous abortion was formulated as a condition for induced abortion. Similarly, considering also the results of a public opinion poll, the minimum age of the woman entitling her to induced abortion at request independent of any other requirement was decreased from 40 to 35 years.

c.   Surveys dealing with psychological factors indicated that direct propaganda for increasing fertility may be counter-productive; i.e. irritating the general public it may have a boomerang effect. Thus, both for promoting the stability of marriages and the development of adequate ideas concerning love, sex, partnership, family life, children, etc., children aged 12-18 are given education on this subject within the framework of the general school system.

d.   The longitudinal surveys indicated that the housing conditions of young couples exert an impact both on desired number of children and especially on actual number of children. It should be mentioned that this problem can be studied only by longitudinal surveys; census and retrospective survey data may be misleading on this subject.
The most important factor is whether the couple has or has not a separate dwelling either at marriage or shortly (within 2-6 years) after marriage, i.e. in the potentially most fertile period. For this reason, housing policy measures give preference to young couples both in the distribution of local council/tenement dwellings and in the allocations of long-term and low interest bank loans for private house building.

e.   Opinions on part-time jobs, children's institutions, child-care allowance, etc. as indicated by the surveys have been considered and, as far as possible, incorporated in the relevant regulations.

As can be seen from the above examples, the dialogue between research workers and policy-makers is an essential precondition for continuous adjustments of the population policy necessitated by new developments.

9.   Government Perspectives and Utilisation of Research for
     Women's and Population Issues in Cyprus
     - Evros I. Demetriades
     Paper reported in Section VI.2

1.   Introduction

     The Government of Cyprus has recognised the value and
usefulness of research in the formulation, implementation, follow-
up and assessment of future perspectives in its economic and
social development efforts.   The complex interrelationships and
linkages that exist between the socio-economic and demographic
aspects of development in a country need to be studied in depth
in order to achieve maximum results from available resources.
     This paper examines where research on such important
issues as population and women's status stands today in Cyprus,
the usefulness of such research, the problems encountered and
attempts to identify topics for further research which will be
useful to the study of such issues.
     The major research undertaken in Cyrpus in the past
decade centred on population, employment status of women and
the socio-economic factors related to female participation.   The
discussion will be based on the experiences derived mainly from
the surveys on Inactive Women, Employment Status of Women
carried out under the auspices of the UNFPA/ILO technical
co-operation project "Population, Employment Planning and Labour
Force Mobility in Cyprus" (CYP/77/PO1) and the multi-round
demographic survey conducted in connection with the UNFPA-
funded project "Comprehensive Population Programme for Cyprus"
(CYP/74/PO1).
     While it is difficult to document the direct utilisation of the
research findings perhaps the most important contribution has
been to create an increased awareness of the importance of
integrating human resource factors into development planning.
Indirect application of the results can be seen in the policies
incorporated into the various Development Plans to improve the
position of women in the labour market, to upgrade child-care
facilities, to reduce the severity of the growing problem of the
educated unemployed and to rectify potential imbalances between
the demand and supply of various skills in the labour market.
Research in these fields has also contributed to the improvement
of the statistical base and to the refinement of data and methodologies.   This includes inter alia a newly-designed sample survey
which laid the foundation for a reliable and cost-effective monthly
time series on employment which is an important tool in human
resources planning.

2.1 Inactive Women Survey

     This survey was prompted by the labour shortage experi-
enced in certain labour intensive exporting industries which

employ mainly women. The purpose was to investigate whether there was a sizeable number of women potentially available for work in selected areas and to what extent and under what conditions they would be willing to work. The findings of the survey were to be passed to manufacturers for study in order to establish factory branches in these regions. The survey was initially launched in two rural regions, comprising 5-10 villages each, with the intention of extending it to other regions in the light of the results and experience acquired in the first stage.

The results showed that there was a reserve of women in the regions studied, of which a proportion could be absorbed if factory branches could be established in the region. However, due to limited telecommunications, transport facilities and other infrastructure, employers were reluctant to invest in remote areas and no such factories were established. Consequently, the survey was not repeated in other parts of the country. Apart from enhancing our knowledge of the reasons why women are not employed and the conditions under which they will be willing to work, the survey results assisted employers in locating women interested to work in the town and thus arrangements were made for their free transportation from their villages to the factories and back.

In assessing the usefulness and problems of this research it can be said that: employers had dramatised their problems of labour shortage and a rather hasty decision was taken for carrying out a survey before determining its cost-effectiveness and necessity. Moreover, employers who would be the main beneficiaries of this study were not asked to contribute to the survey budget and this prompted them to request a repetition of the survey in other regions of the country. Had they been asked to contribute to the budget, most likely they would have studied the matter more seriously and their belated concern about limited or no infrastructure would have been expressed before the survey was launched and the Government would have acted accordingly. Their financial contribution would thus have been the barometer for the genuineness of their intentions. This experience suggests that before embarking on any research, the cost-effectiveness and the usefulness of the survey results should be carefully assessed.

2.2   Employment Status of Women Survey

This survey aimed at analysing the employment status of women versus that of men and the underlying factors that affect women's participation in the labour force. It consisted of two enquiries: namely the employers' survey and the employees' survey. The former aimed at exploring the recruitment, training, promotion and pay practices of employers while the second enquiry on employees focused on the work history, problems, attitudes about work and fertility history of working women (see House, 1982 and 1983 for detailed results).

The survey provided rich information on many aspects of

the employment status of women and in particular it demonstrated the occupational segregation and pay differentials between the two sexes. The research results were used to suggest ways and means of improving women's position and provided the basis for the preparation of the relevant section of the new Development Plan. Since the Government's explicit policy is to halt the long-term decline in fertility, while at the same time, to raise female labour force activity rates, the main issue is how to construct a social and economic environment in which married women find wage employment and domestic responsibilities to be reasonably compatible. Such an environment could be initiated by some form of equal opportunity legislation, adoption of legislation guaranteeing the right of working women to paid maternity leave and protection from dismissal during pregnancy and childbirth; introduction of flexible working hours, nursing breaks, etc. This research has also pointed out that in-depth assessment of the use and adequacy of exising child-care facilities is needed. The problem of caring for school-age children of working mothers needs further attention and study.

2.3   Multi-round Demographic Survey (M-RDS)

This survey aimed at providing further knowledge on the dynamics of population, on the interrelationships between demographic and socio-economic variables, as well as creating an awareness of the importance of demographic changes in socio-economic development which must be taken into consideration in the formulation of a population policy. In particular, the M-RDS was designed to provide data on the levels, trends and determinants of fertility, mortality and internal migration and to shed light on the interaction between demographic characteristics and socio-economic variables such as employment, social class, education level, etc. The survey provided abundant data on the above topics which enhanced our knowledge in the very important, but little explored in the past, dynamics of population change. The results have been extensively utilised by various Government departments in the formulation of measures and policies in connection with population and welfare issues.

The survey has documented a negative association of fertility with urban place of residence, educational levels of both husband and wife, higher social class and employment of women. It must be pointed out, however, that in the formulation of a population policy, measures and incentives to increase fertility, great care must be taken on the direction of cause to effect relationships. For instance, the established relationship of negative association of fertility with variables such as urban residence, level of education, etc. cannot in any way imply direct causation. Experience from developed countries with pro-natalist policies supports the notion that once fertility has reached low levels the trend cannot be reversed, apart from trivial changes, regardless of measures and incentives that might be adopted.

An important finding of both the Multi-round Demographic Survey and the Survey on the Employment Status of Women, is that participation of women in the labour market is negatively correlated with fertility. Given the policies of the Government aiming at increasing both the female participation and the level of fertility, a contradiction has been identified. This was recognised as a matter needing measures to alleviate the effects of the apparent conflict.

2.4 National Workshop on Population and Employment Issues

A significant contribution of the research programme in Cyprus was the organisation of a National Workshop on Population, Employment Planning and Labour Force Mobility in order to disseminate the findings of research in employment and population fields to a wide audience of government officials connected with such issues, trade unions and employers.

This research has contributed significantly to the better understanding and knowledge base of the interaction between the demographic and socio-economic variables in the development process. It highlighted the importance of integrating population employment and related policies into national development planning and provided the basis for further research into the development of human resources in Cyprus which are considered an important variable in efforts to sustain and accelerate social and economic development. The overwhelming assessment was that the proceedings of the workshop were extremely useful and additional gatherings of this nature should be promoted in the future. The workshop stressed the usefulness of dissemination of such findings and of obtaining feedback information from a wider spectrum of users.

3. Methods of Increasing Utilisation of Research

In order to increase the utilisation of research the following methods are suggested:

(i)   Setting of clear and specific objectives of research. There is often a tendency to incorporate too many topics in an inquiry and this should be avoided as it increases costs and reduces the quality of the replies;

(ii)   Specific objectives can be achieved better by bringing together at the planning stage of a study, potential users and researchers for discussing the issues to be examined;

(iii)   Dissemination of research findings to a wider spectrum of possible users. This will enable potential users to know about the existence of information relevant to their work and develop a link for exchange of ideas for the improvement of research between users and researchers; and

(iv)   Close co-operation between research workers and policy-makers in the process of the formulation, implementation and monitoring of policy measures.

4. Future Research Activities

Women represent the component of the labour force whose participation is most sensitive to economic and social pressures. Therefore, the implications of the level and pattern of labour force participation on fertility, population growth, family decision-making, skill development, the allocation of education resources, level of unemployment, rural-urban migration, wage rates, wage differentials and income distribution, are topics needing further exploration.

Further research is required on child-care institutions. The existing situation as well as the views of both working and not working mothers on this issue are of utmost importance in encouraging more women into the labour force or in pursuing and monitoring an employment policy.

Before embarking on a population policy it would be useful to have the views and attitudes of the public on population matters. After all, it is what people think on family size that determines their fertility behaviour. Moreover population policy has wide social and economic ramifications and further studies and investigations of the various policy issues will be invaluable to the Government in formulating new legislation and measures.

For the more rational distribution of the labour force the determinants of labour mobility within sectors, occupations and regions needs to be studied in depth. This would entail the specification of a structural model which captures both a function representing the demand by firms for workers to switch from one occupation or industry to another, as well as a function representing the demand by workers for such movement.

A continuous flow of up-to-date, consistent and comparable information is needed for research findings to be instrumental in policy formulation and monitoring. The National Household Survey Capability Programme of the UN provides this framework and Cyprus is in the process of implementing such a programme.

In view of the increasing recognition of the importance of income distributional aspects of wage and employment policies, analysis and assessment of these interlinkages are considered essential.

Given the drain of scarce human resources by past out-migration, the determinants and consequences of this migration for economic and social development need to be identified with a view to designing a comprehensive population and employment strategy for the country. Increasing urbanisation and the consequent large depopulation of rural areas as well as the future regional patterns of economic development necessitates the initiation of studies as a means of understanding internal migratory movements in order to design future population and employment policies.

Current manpower planning exercises in Cyprus, as in many other countries, use the traditional "labour requirements" approach, whereby the matrix of labour coefficients is assumed to be unchanged over time. However, the technique has been the subject of a great deal of criticism by labour economists because it does not allow for substitution possibilities amongst skills in production. On the other hand, theoretical and empirical developments of alternative approaches are still in their infancy. While the initial task is to develop a matrix of labour requirements per unit of output for at least two separate points in time, the much more demanding problem is to explain any changes that may have occurred in these labour coefficients. Clearly, for planning purposes, it is not enough simply to know that there have been changes in the matrix but it is essential to identify the determinants of these changes, some of which may be amendable to policy manipulation.

Finally, although a substantial amount of research is underway in labour absorption and other aspects of employment in developing countries, a standard methodology needs to be developed for assessing trends in sectoral employment growth, the factors contributing to these trends and the outlook for employment.

References

House, W.J. 1981. *Patterns and determinants of female labour force participation in Cyprus*, ILO/UNFPA project CYP/77/PO1, working paper no. 8. Nicosia, Department of Statistics and Research, Republic of Cyprus.

---. 1982a. *Demographic aspects of labour mobility in Cyprus*, ILO/ UNFPA project, CYP/77/PO1, working paper no. 7. Nicosia, Department of Statistics and Research, Republic of Cyprus.

---. 1982b. *Socio-economic determinants of fertility in Cyprus*. Geneva, ILO; mimeographed World Employment Programme research working paper.

---. 1983a. *Discrimination and segregation of women workers in Cyprus*, ILO/UNFPA Project CYP/77/PO1, Report no. 17. Nicosia, Department of Statistics and Research, Republic of Cyprus.

---. 1983b. "Occupational segregation and discriminatory pay: The position of women in the Cyprus labour market", in *International Labour Review*. Geneva, ILO.

Republic of Cyprus, Department of Statistics and Research. 1982. *Proceedings of the National Workshop on the UNFPA/ ILO Project CYP/77/PO1: Population, Employment Planning and Labour Force Mobility in Cyprus*, Report no. 2. Nicosia.

---. 1983a. "Multi-round demographic survey, 198071981", Main Report (preliminary issue). Nicosia.

---. 1983b. *Survey on the employment status of women in Cyprus*, ILO/UNFPA project CYP/77/PO1, Report no. 18. Nicosia.

Stylianou, O. 1982. "The status of Cypriot women in the labour force", in Republic of Cyprus, Department of Statistics and Research: *Proceedings of the National Workshop on the UNFPA/ILO Project CYP/77/PO1*. Nicosia.

10.   Women, Work and Fertility in Uzbekistan[1]

At present, the Uzbek Soviet Socialist Republic is an economically developed republic of the USSR with a highly efficient agriculture, a developed modern industry and infrastructure, and a high rate of economic growth. From 1970 to 1979, the average annual rates of growth in the national income were 5.2 per cent for the USSR and 6.0 per cent for the Uzbek Republic. Total industrial output in Uzbekistan in 1979 had increased fifteenfold since 1940, while gross agricultural output was 436 per cent of the 1940 level.

In 1982, the population of the Republic was 16.6 million with 58 per cent living in rural areas. The capital city, Tashkent, has a population of almost two million persons.

The general level of fertility in Uzbekistan grew from about 1950 until the late-1960s and was then followed by a decline (see table 1).

Table 1:   Age specific fertility rates (per thousand) and total fertility rate in the Uzbek Republic, 1958-1979*

Years	Age of women (years)							Total fertility rate
	15-19	20-24	25-29	30-34	35-39	40-44	45-49	
1958-59	38.3	209.9	240.7	206.7	178.6	96.8	38.4	5.04
1965-66	30.2	252.8	270.2	238.1	181.3	99.2	41.0	5.56
1969-70	41.7	261.3	265.3	245.6	194.9	91.5	27.0	5.64
1972-73	39.9	280.0	287.0	234.1	187.0	87.6	17.6	5.67
1075-76	39.1	279.0	301.3	225.2	170.6	82.0	16.8	5.57
1978-79	35.4	277.3	281.7	210.7	134.7	66.9	12.5	5.10

Note: * The total fertility rate estimates the average number of children which would be born to a women throughout her child-bearing years if she experienced the current age-specific fertility rates.

Source: Population of the USSR 1973,   p.   137;   Bulletin of Statistics, 1977, No. 11 and 1980, No. 11.

An analysis of age-specific fertility rates reveals that the decline started in the mid-1960s for women 40 years and over and in the early 1970s for women in their thirties and women less than age 20 years. Only recently has there been a slight decline in fertility for women in their twenties. The decline of fertility in the 15-19 age group seems to indicate a reduction in the number of early marriages.

There are, however, wide differences in birth rates between rural and urban areas. For example, the crude birth rate of the rural population in 1977 was 38.9 per thousand compared to 19.2 in Tashkent in 1979.

Such notable regional divergences result from substantial differences in reproductive behaviour amongst the nationalities comprising the Republic. In 1979, the crude birth rate within Uzbekistan was 38.5 per thousand for Uzbeks, 16.5 for Turkmens, 33.6 for Kirghiz and 42.7 for Kara-Kalpaks. The high birth rate among Uzbeks and other indigenous groups reflects the desire for large families - about five or six children. The ideal family size appears to be somewhat less in the younger generation. Interviews with rural women conducted in 1978 by the Population Research Laboratory of Tashkent University indicated an ideal of 5.1 for women aged 18-22 years as compared to 6.6 for women in the 43-47 age group.

Educational levels have risen rapidly in the Uzbek Republic and the levels for women compare well with those for men and with those for all women in the USSR. For example in the Uzbek SSR in 1979, 38 per cent of women over 10 years of age had completed secondary or higher education compared to 46.4 per cent of the men and 38.3 per cent of all women in the USSR (Bulletin of Statistics, 1980).

Table 2: Average expected number of children in high birth rate nationalities of the USSR* according to level of marriage cohort and education level, 1972

Year of marriage	Women's educational level		
	Incomplete secondary	Secondary and secondary specialised	Higher and incomplete higher
1940-1944	5.95	5.27	4.05
1960-1964	5.87	5.35	4.05
1965-1969	5.11	4.74	3.65

* Uzbek, Turkmen, Tajik, Kirghiz, Kazakh and Azerbaijan women.

Source: How many children will there be in the Soviet family?, 1977, p. 66.

Data suggest that women with higher levels of education have fewer children. The results of a survey conducted in 1972 among high fertility nationalities in the USSR (see table 2) indicated very substantial differences in the average expected number of children (and thus in the aggregated birth rates of

the age cohorts) according to level of education. Rising educational levels may partly explain recent declines in the fertility
rates. This implies that in the future in Uzbekistan, a further
reduction in the birth rates can be expected.

A high female labour force participation rate is one of the
major features of the socio-economic development of the Uzbek
Republic and of the Soviet Union as a whole. The share of
women in the total workforce of the Uzbek Republic was 43 per
cent in 1980 and 1981 (Bulletin of Statistics, 1982, p. 69).

Forty-two per cent of office and factory workers were
women in 1979 compared to 51 per cent in the USSR (The
national economy of the USSR in 1979). In 1970, 77 per cent of
the women aged 16 to 54 were economically active (Ubaidullayeva,
1979). Table 3 shows women's share of employment in the
various branches of the Uzbek national economy in 1970.

Figures for 1970-73 (Ubaidullayeva, 1979, p. 65) indicate
that women in Uzbekistan constitute a high proportion of certain
specialists with higher or specialised secondary education: 58.0
per cent of doctors, 45.6 per cent of economists and planners,
28.3 per cent of engineers and 49.3 per cent of teachers and
librarians.

Table 3: Percentage of Uzbek labour force which is female
by branches of the national economy

Branch	Percentage women
Industry, construction, transport and communication	33.3
Agriculture and forestry	54.5
Trade, technical supplies and marketing	44.5
Education, science and health	60.3
Housing, communal utilities, services, etc.	47.8

Source: The results of the USSR population census of 1970,
Vol. V, pp. 224-229).

These various facts and figures concerning Uzbekistan have
been presented to document that relatively high levels of fertility
continue to exist despite high educational levels of women and
their high rate of participation in the labour force.

The Uzbek population, with a short but intensive period of
development, has retained its traditional demographic patterns
for longer than elsewhere. It is possible that policy measures
such as child allowances, special allowances to large families, and
the construction of day care centres subsidised by the state
have contributed to maintaining high fertility levels. Neverthe-

less, it is likely that the recent trends towards lower fertility will continue along with continued social and economic development.

Notes:

[1] This paper draws on the papers presented at the seminar by I. Mulliadjanov and M.R. Buryeva as well as the chapter "Uzbek Soviet Socialist Republic" by A. Ya Kvasha, A.P. Sudoplatov, A.B. Ata-Mirzaev, I.L. Kalinyuk, V.M. Moiseenko, R.A. Ubaidullayeva in the forthcoming book edited by Bodrova and Anker, Working women in socialist countries: The fertility connection.

References:

Itogi Vsesoyuznoi perepisi naseleniya 1970g [The results of the USSR national population census of 1970], Vol. III. Moscow.

Narodnoye khozyaistvo SSR v 1979 godu [The national economy of the USSR in 1979]. Moscow.

Naseleniye SSSR v 1973 godu [Population of the USSR 1973]. Moscow.

Skolko detei budet v sovetskoi semye? [How many children will there be in the soviet family?]

Ubaidullayeva, R.A. 1979. *Trudovye resursy i effektivnost ikh ispolzovaniya* [Labour resources and the effectiveness of their utilisation]. Tashkent.

Vestnik statistiki [Bulletin of statistics], 1977, 1980, 1982.

APPENDIX 1

List of Participants

Bangladesh

CHISTY Meher Negar Nur Elahi
      Senior Officer,
Ministry of Social Welfare and
Women's Affairs,
Government of Bangladesh,
Dhaka

ELAHI K. Maumood
      Chairman and Associate
Professor,
Department of Geography,
Jahagirnagar University,
Dhaka

Brazil

GARCIA CASTRO Mary
      Research Scholar,
Centre for Latin American
Studies,
University of Florida,
Gainesville, USA;
C.N.P.Q. Brazilian Government
Fellow

Bulgaria

MIKHAILOVA Pavlina
      Research Scholar, Ph.D.
Institute of Sociology,
Bulgarian Academy of Sciences,
Sofia

Canada

HEIN Catherine
      Research Scholar,
Consultant, ILO Geneva
Rapporteur of the seminar

Cuba

ALVAREZ-LAJONCHERE Celestino
      Direccion Nacional,
Federation of Cuban Women,
Havana;
Grupo Nacional Trabajo Educ.
Sexual (GNTES) Cuba

FARNOS, Alfonso

Dean of Economic Faculty,
Havana University;
Professor of Demographic
Research Centre, Havana

Cyprus

DEMETRIADES Evros

Director,
Department of Statistics and
Research,
Ministry of Finance, Nicosia

Czechoslovakia

PAVLIK Zdenek

Associate Professor of
Demography,
Charles University, Faculty of
Sciences;
President of the Czechoslovak
Demographic Society, Prague

Egypt

SHOUKRY, Aliaa Ali

Professor of Anthropology,
Head of Department of
Sociology and Anthropology,
Ain Shams University for
Girls, Cairo

Hungary

MILTENYI Karoly

Deputy Head,
Social Statistics Department,
Hungarian Central Statistical
Office, Budapest

India

KHAN, Mohamad Ejazuddin

Associate Director,
Operations Research Group,
New Delhi

Jordan

ABDUL BAQI Nawal

Ministry of Labour, Amman

Nigeria

ADEOKUN Lawrence A.

Research Scholar,
Department of Demography and
Social Statistics,
University of Ife, Ile-Ife

Pakistan

INAYATULLAH Attiya

Adviser to the President and
Minister of State for
Population Planning
Government of Pakistan,
Islamabad

USA

MUELLER Eva

Professor of Economics,
Population Studies Center,
University of Michigan, Ann
Arbor

USSR

MAKHMUDOVA Naima

President,
Uzbek Republican Trade Union
Council

KANAYEV Georguy

Deputy Head,
International Department,
All-Union Central Council of
Trade Unions (AUCCTU)

TASHMATOV Akram

Secretary,
Uzbek Republican Trade Union
Council

BRAILOV Anatoly

President,
Tashkent Regional Trade Union
Council

BODROVA Valentina

Ph.D. in Economics,
Senior Research Scholar,
Population Centre, Moscow
University

MULLIADJANOV Iskhak

Ph.D. in Economics,
Director,
Centre for Scientific Labour
Organisation,
Uzbekistan Republican State
Planning Committee

TATEVOSOV Rudolf

Ph.D. in Geographic Sciences,
Chief, Department of Economics
of Population and Social and
Demographic Development,
Population Centre,
Moscow University

BURIEVA Mamlakat	Research Scholar, Tashkent University
TURCHANINOVA Svetlana	Ph.D. in Economics, Senior Research Scholar, Research Department, Shvernik Higher Trade Union School
PERVOUCHINE Alexandre S.	Ph.D. in Economics, Chief, Section for Studies of Foreign Population Issues; Deputy Chief, Population Centre, Moscow University
MARKOV Vladimir	Ph.D. in Economics, Assistant Head of the Social and Demographic Department, Gosplan, USSR
DMITRIEVA Rimma	Ph.D. in Economics, Chief, Population Statistics Department, Central Statistical Board, USSR
MITYAEV Ivan	Section Chief, AUCCTU International Department

People's Democratic Republic of Yemen

SALEH Noor Alhuda	Chief, Co-operation Department, Ministry of Planning, Aden

Worker Consultants

ALAGAWADI Usha	All-India Trade Union Congress, New Delhi
NARGIS Makhduma	Bangladesh Trade Union Kendra, Dhaka

International Labour Organisation (ILO)

DOCTOR Kailas C.	Chief, Population and Labour Policies Branch, EMP/POP

SMIRNOVA Raissa

Chief,
Office for Women Workers'
Questions

KORNILOV Stanislav

Deputy Director,
ILO Office in Moscow

ANKER Richard

Project Manager,
Demographic Change and the
Role of Women, EMP/POP

FAROOQ Ghazi M.

Senior Population Economist,
EMP/POP

OPPONG Christine

Senior Anthropological
Research Officer, EMP/POP

PANKOV Valery

Senior Research Officer,
Employment and Manpower
Planning Branch

SCHAEFER Ute

Secretary, EMP/POP

DATE-BAH Eugenia

ILO Regional Office for Africa,
Addis Ababa

APPENDIX 2

Seminar Programme

Sunday, 9 October

10.00-12.30   Tour of Moscow, Kremlin and Underground included.
Lay wreaths on V.I. Lenin's Mausoleum and Tomb of Unknown Soldier

Monday, 10 October

Travel to Tashkent

Tuesday, 11 October

09.15   Lay wreaths on V.I. Lenin's Monument

10.00-11.00   Opening of the Seminar
Addresses of welcome by the Council of Ministers of the Uzbek SSR, City Council, Uzbek Republic Trade Union Council and international organisations. Mrs. N.M. Makhmudova, President of the Uzbek Republic Trade Union Council will be in the chair. The Seminar will be held in Cooperator's House.

11.00-11.30   Introduction of participants
Discussion of organisational matters
Overview - R. Anker

14.00-17.00   Session I: Women's Economic Contribution and Demographic Change: Measuring the Female Labour Force and Other Methodological Issues

        (a)   Female labour force participation: Conceptual and measurement difficulties - R. Anker

        (b)   Usefulness of qualitative approaches - C. Oppong

        (c)   Methodological insights from collaborative Indian studies - M.E. Khan

        Discussants: E. Mueller
                         L. Adeokun

| 17.00-18.30 | Sightseeing tour of Tashkent |

| 18.30-19.00 | Uzbekistan National Theatre |

Wednesday, 12 October

09.30-12.30   Session II: Women's Economic Contributions and Opportunities: Rural Case Studies

    (a)   An internationally assisted handloom programme in India - M.E. Khan

    (b)   Government programmes for women in Bangladeshi villages - K.M. Elahi

    (c)   Women in Egyptian villages - A.A. Shoukry

    Discussants: A. Inayatullah
                  E. Date-Bah

14.00-17.30   Session III: Women's Economic Contributions: Urban Case Studies

    (a)   Tapping the female labour reserve in Cyprus - E. Demetriades

    (b)   Export promotion zones in Mauritius - C. Hein

    (c)   Women's work in a Ghanaian city - E. Date-Bah

    (d)   Women's work in a Nigerian city - L. Adeokun

    Discussant: M. Garcia Castro

18.30   Concert of amateur performers to be held in Aircraft Industry Workers' Palace of Culture

Thursday, 13 October

09.30-12.30   Session IV: Women's Roles, Fertility and Family Planning in High Fertility Areas

    (a)   Family planning acceptance and women's programmes in Bangladeshi villages - K.M. Elahi

	(b)	Evidence of change from Nigeria and Ghana - C. Oppong
	(c)	Women and health programmes in India - M.E. Khan

Discussants: M. Nargis
                           G.M. Farooq

14.30-17.30   (d)   A study of fertility in the Uzbek SSR
                         - M.R. Burieva
                         Stability of the high birth rate in
                         Uzbekistan - I. Mulliadjanov

                  (e)   Fertility and changing family structure in
                         Bogota, Colombia - M. Garcia Castro

                  (f)   Demographic transition in Cuba and economic
                         and social roles of women - A. Farnos

                  (g)   Sex education in Cuba
                         - C. Alvarez-Lajonchere

Discussants: V. Bodrova
                             G.M. Farooq

18.00   Exhibition of Economic Achievements

Friday, 14 October

09.30-12.30   Session V: Fertility and Female Employment in
                      Low Fertility Socialist Countries: Determinants
                      and Policies

                  (a)   Hungary - K. Miltenyi

                  (b)   Czechoslovakia - Z. Pavlik

                  (c)   USSR - S. Turchaninova

                  (d)   Cuba - A. Farnos

                  (e)   Bulgaria - P. Mikhailova

Discussants: E. Mueller
                             Z. Pavlik

15.00-16.00   Talk in the Supreme Council of the Uzbek SSR

16.30-18.30   Visit to the Central Asian Ecclesiastical Board

Saturday, 15 October

09.30-12.30   Session VI: <u>Information for Policy Formulation:</u> <u>Agency and Trade Union Perspectives on Utilis-</u> <u>ation of Research for Women's and Population</u> <u>Issues</u>

         (a)   UNFPA programme - K.C. Doctor

         (b)   ILO programme on women workers' questions R. Smirnova

         (c)   Women's issues from the perspective of the ILO's population programme - K.C. Doctor

         (d)   Research for policy formulation in high fertility LDCs - E. Mueller

         (e)   Soviet trade union activities to improve position of working women - S. Turchaninova

         (f)   Bangladeshi trade unions - M. Nargis

         (g)   Indian trade unions - U. Alagawadi

         Discussants: A. Inayatullah
                              E. Demetriades

14.30-17.30   Session VII: <u>Information for Policy Formulation:</u> <u>Government Perspectives on Utilisation of</u> <u>Research for Women's and Population Issues</u>

         (a)   Pakistan - A. Inayatullah

         (b)   Bangladesh - M. Chisty

         (c)   Soviet Union - R. Dmitrieva

         (d)   Cuba - C. Alvarez-Lajonchere

         (e)   Cyprus - E. Demetriades

         (f)   Jordan - N. Abdul Baqi

         (g)   PDRY - N. Saleh

         (h)   Hungary - K. Miltenyi

(i)   Bulgaria - P. Mikhailova

19.00-21.00   Cultural programme

Sunday, 16 October

Visit to Samarkand

Monday, 17 October

09.30-12.00   Plenary session and formation of drafting committee to prepare conclusions and recommendations

14.30-17.00   Continuation of drafting committee session

Tuesday, 18 October

10.00-13.00   Visit to Clothing Factories Association Krasnaya Zarya for Group 1 to see production, talk with management and trade union activists, visit kindergarten

Visit to Artistic Goods Factory for Group 2 to see production, talk with management and trade union activists, observe labour conditions of a woman home-worker

Visit to Midwifery and Gynaecology Institute

15.00-18.00   Presentation and Discussion of Drafting Committee Report

19.00   Performance in A. Navoi Theatre

Wednesday, 19 October

09.30-12.30   Presentation and Discussion of Drafting Committee Report (continued)

14.30-17.00   Closing of Seminar

Thursday, 20 October (optional)

10.00-15.00   Trip to collective or state farm in Tashkent area to talk with management, see production and social and welfare facilities.

<u>Friday, 21 October: Return to Moscow</u>

10.10   Travel to Moscow.

15.30-18.00   Meeting   with   Mrs.   Alexandra   Biryukova,
                    Secretary of the AUCCTU

APPENDIX 3

BIBLIOGRAPHY OF RELEVANT ILO PUBLICATIONS

Adeokun, L.A.; Adepoju, A.; Ilori, F.A.; Adewuyi, A.A.; Ebigbola, J.A. 1984. *The Ife labour market: A Nigerian case study*. Geneva, ILO; mimeographed World Employment Programme research working paper.

Akuffo, F.O. Forthcoming. "Teenage pregnancies and school dropouts: The relevance of family life education and vocational training to girls' employment opportunities", in C. Oppong (ed.): *Sex roles, population and development in West Africa: Research and policy issues*.

Anker, R. 1980. *Research on women's roles and demographic change: Survey questionnaires for households, women, men and communities with background explanations*. Geneva, ILO.

---. 1983a. "Female labour definitions and labour force participation in developing countries: A critique of current data collection techniques", in *International Labour Review* (Geneva, ILO), Nov-Dec, Vol. 122, No. 6.

---. 1983b. *Measuring female labour force participation in developing countries: Description of an experimental field test of questionnaire types, sex of interviewer and respondent types*. Geneva, ILO; mimeographed World Employment Programme research working paper.

Anker, R.; Anker, M. 1982. *Reproductive behaviour in households of rural Gujarat: Social, economic and community factors*. New Delhi, Concept Publishing Co.

Anker, R.; Buvinic, M.; Youssef, N. (eds.) 1982. *Inter-actions between women's roles and population trends in the Third World*. London, Croom Helm.

Anker, R.; Hein, C. (eds.) Forthcoming. *Sex segregation and discrimination in urban labour markets of Third World countries*.

Anker, R.; Knowles, J.C. 1982. *The determinants of fertility in developing countries: A case study of Kenya*. Liège, Ordina.

Barta, B.; Klinger, A.; Miltényi, K.; Vukovich, G. 1983. *Interdependence between female employment and fertility in Hungary*. Geneva, ILO; mimeographed World Employment Programme research working paper.

---. 1984. *Fertility, female employment and policy measures in*

Hungary, Women, Work and Development Series No. 6. Geneva, ILO.

Bleek, W. Forthcoming. "Family and family planning in Southern Ghana", in C. Oppong (ed.): *Sex roles, population and development in West Africa: Research and policy issues*.

Bodrova, V.; Anker, R. Forthcoming. *Working women in socialist countries: The fertility connection*. Geneva, ILO.

Date-Bah, E. 1982. *Sex inequality in an African urban labour market: The case of Accra-Tema*. Geneva, ILO; mimeographed World Employment Programme research working paper.

Deere, C.D.; León de Leal, M. 1982. *Women in Andean agriculture*, Women, Work and Development series, No. 4. Geneva, ILO.

Farnos, A.; Gonzales, F.; Hernandez. R. 1983. *The role of women and demographic changes in Cuba*. Geneva, ILO; mimeographed World Employment Programme research working paper.

Farooq, G.; Ekanem, I.; Ojelade, M.A. Forthcoming. "Family size preferences and fertility in South Western Nigeria", in C. Oppong (ed.): *Sex roles, population and development in West Africa: Research and policy issues*.

Goldschmidt-Clermont, L. 1982. *Unpaid work in the household. A review of economic evaluation methods*, Women, Work and Development series No. 1. Geneva, ILO.

Gulati, L. 1983. *Women in fishing villages on the Kerala coast: Demographic and socio-economic impacts of a fisheries development project*. Geneva, ILO; mimeographed World Employment Programme research working paper.

---. In press. *Demographic and socio-economic impact of a fisheries project: Women in three fishing villages on the Kerala coast*, Women, Work and Development series. Geneva, ILO.

Hein, C. 1981. *Employment of women in Mauritian industry: Opportunity or exploitation?* Geneva, ILO; mimeographed World Employment Programme research working paper.

---. 1982. *Factory employment, marriage and fertility: The case of women in Mauritius*. Geneva, ILO; mimeographed World Employment Programme research working paper.

---. 1984. "Jobs for the girls: Export manufacturing in Mauritius", in *International Labour Review* (Geneva, ILO),

Mar-Apr, Vol. 123, No. 2.

House, W.J. 1982a. *Patterns and determinants of female labour force participation in Cyprus*. Geneva, ILO; mimeographed World Employment Programme research working paper.

---. 1982b. *Labour market segmentation: Evidence from Cyprus*. Geneva, ILO; mimeographed World Employment Programme research working paper.

---. 1983. "Occupational segregation and discriminatory pay: The position of women in the Cyprus labour market", in *International Labour Review* (Geneva, ILO), Jan-Feb, Vol. 112, No. 1.

ILO. 1980a. *Women's participation in the economic activity of the world (statistical analysis)*. Geneva, ILO.

---. 1980b. *Women's participation in the economic and social activities in the USSR and European socialist countries (statistical analysis)*. Geneva, ILO.

---. 1983. *Report of the International Labour Organisation on its Activities of Special Interest to Women*, document prepared by the Office for Women Workers' Questions. Geneva, ILO.

Kurian, R. 1982. *Women workers in the Sri Lanka plantation sector*, Women, Work and Development series No. 5. Geneva, ILO.

Lynch, P. with Fahmy, H. 1983. *Craftswomen in Kerdassa, Egypt: Household production and reproduction*. Geneva, ILO; mimeographed World Employment Progarmme research working paper.

---. 1984. *Craftswomen in Kerdassa, Egypt: Household production and reproduction*, Women, Work and Development series. Geneva, ILO.

Molyneux, M. 1982. *State policies and the position of women workers in the People's Democratic Republic of Yemen between 1967 and 1977*, Women, Work and Development series No. 3. Geneva, ILO.

Nag, M.; Anker, R.; Khan, M.E. 1982. *A guide to anthropological study of women's roles and demographic change in India.* Geneva, ILO; mimeographed World Employment Programme research working paper.

Oppong, C. 1979. *Family structure and women's reproductive and productive roles: Some conceptual and methodological issues.* Geneva, ILO; mimeographed World Employment

Programme research working paper.

---. 1980. *A synopsis of seven roles and status of women: An outline of a conceptual and methodological approach.* Geneva, ILO; mimeographed World Employment Programme research working paper.

---. 1982a. *Maternal role rewards, opportunity costs and fertility.* Geneva, ILO; mimeographed World Employment Programme research working paper.

---. 1982b. *Reproduction and resources: Some anthropological evidence from Ghana.* Geneva, ILO; mimeographed World Employment Programme research working paper.

---. 1982c. *Familial roles and fertility: Some labour policy aspects.* Geneva. ILO; mimeographed World Employment Programme research working paper.

---. 1983. *Paternal costs, role strain and fertility regulation: Some Ghanaian evidence.* Geneva, ILO; mimeographed World Employment Programme research working paper.

---. (ed.) Forthcoming. *Sex roles, population and development in West Africa: Research and policy issues.*

Oppong, C.; Abu, K. 1984. *The changing maternal role of Ghanaian women: Education, migration and employment.* Geneva, ILO; mimeographed World Employment Programme research working paper.

Oppong, C.; Church, K. 1981. *A field guide to research on seven roles of women: Focussed biographies.* Geneva, ILO; mimeographed World Employment Programme research working paper.

Oppong, C.; Haavio-Mannila, E. 1979. "Women, population and development", in P. Hauser (ed.): *World population and development: Challenges and prospects.* Syracuse University Press, UNFPA.

Orubuloye, I. Forthcoming. "Values and costs of daughters and sons to Yoruba mothers and fathers", in C. Oppong (ed.): *Sex roles, population and development in West Africa: Research and policy issues.*

Papola, T.S. 1983. *Women workers in an Indian urban labour market.* Geneva, ILO; mimeographed World Employment Programme research working paper.

Pasuk Phongpaichig. 1982. *From peasant girls to Bangkok masseuses,* Women, Work and Development series No. 2.

Geneva, ILO.

Pittin, R. 1982. *Documentation of women's work in Nigeria: Problems and solutions*. Geneva, ILO; mimeographed World Employment Programme research working paper.

Standing, G. 1978. *Labour force participation and development*. Geneva, ILO.

---. 1981. *Unemployment and female labour: A study of labour supply in Kingston, Jamaica*. London, Macmillan.

Standing, G.; Sheehan, G. 1977. *Labour force participation in low-income countries*. Geneva, ILO.

www.ingramcontent.com/pod-product-compliance
Lightning Source LLC
Chambersburg PA
CBHW071836200326
41519CB00016B/4135